Gloriously
GLUTEN FREE

hamlyn

Gloriously GLUTEN FREE

Fresh & simple
gluten-free recipes
for healthy eating
every day

SUSANNA
BOOTH

Contents

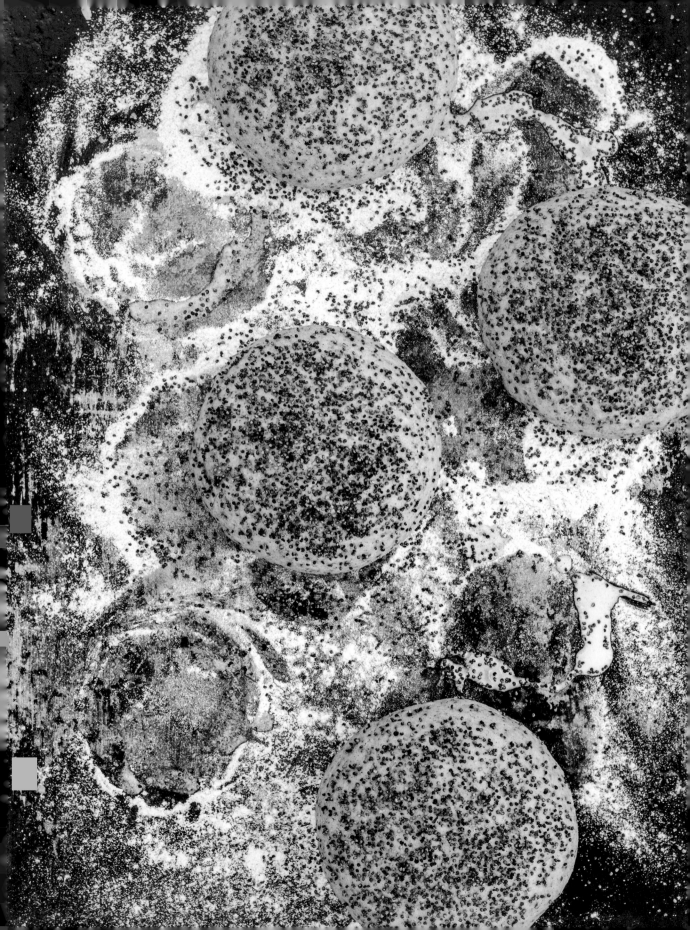

Introduction

Gluten-free lifestyles are increasingly popular, but trying to make gluten-free alternatives to the recipes you love can be a challenge. This is because gluten is a rather special molecule – it is the gluten that makes wheat-based cookery so diverse, from flaky pastries to airy muffins or crunchy, chewy pizzas.

However, if you've so far been dispirited by dense, gritty gluten-free foods, then this is the book you have been waiting for. I have used my science background to take an inventive new look at cooking without gluten. This collection of recipes ranges from the simple to the seductive, but in each case I have chosen the cooking method that will produce the finest possible results: dishes that will delight anyone, regardless of whether they can eat gluten or not. And if you need recipes to suit other requirements as well (like dairy-free, egg-free, nut-free or vegan), just turn to my Recipe Finder on pages 12–13.

Because gluten-free flours behave differently to wheat flours, merely replacing wheat flour with gluten-free flour in recipes rarely yields the expected outcome. In fact, I found the best results came from thinking about my cookery in a very logical and scientific way. This means some of the methods will be different to those you are used to. For instance, my pre-cooking technique allows you to make (among other things) delicate crêpes, a self-saucing hot chocolate pudding and soft vanilla sponge. My new technique for yeast cookery produces moreish cinnamon spiral buns, thin-crust pizza and seeded buckwheat rolls. Meanwhile, a simple yet delicious and robust pastry is used in anything from dainty glazed fruit tartlets and pumpkin pie to broccoli and bacon quiche. Gluten-free cooking has to use different methods to get the best results – I'm delighted to share them with you in the pages of this book.

Susanna Booth

Information about Gluten-free Diets

WHAT IS GLUTEN?

Gluten is a complex protein found in wheat, bulgar wheat, couscous, durum wheat, einkorn, emmer, farro, khorasan wheat (Kamut®), semolina, spelt and triticale. Barley and rye contain related proteins, while oats are also to be avoided because they are so commonly contaminated during growing and/or processing (gluten-free oats are available, but consult a dietitian before including oats in your diet because they can cause problems for some individuals).

A gluten-free diet can be beneficial for many reasons. Up to 1 in 100 people is estimated to suffer from coeliac disease, a permanent autoimmune condition that causes the body to react when it senses even the tiniest amount of gluten, resulting in painful inflammation and damage to the lining of the small intestine. Complete abstinence from gluten is the only effective treatment for this condition. A small number of people are allergic to wheat, barley or rye. In this instance, the sufferer's body releases a chemical called histamine that can lead to a range of symptoms ranging from itchy eyes, rashes or sneezing to anaphylactic shock in severe cases. Or you may be among those people who are sensitive or intolerant to gluten, finding that you simply feel better when you don't eat foods containing it.

If you are choosing to go completely gluten-free, it is important to consult your healthcare provider and/or a qualified dietitian before you eliminate gluten from your diet. Wheat flour, especially wholemeal wheat flour, contains fibre, B vitamins and calcium. Wheat-based products may also be fortified with vitamins and minerals, like iron. It is important to consider this and to plan your meals carefully – the recipes in this book are not intended to form a balanced diet in themselves.

CHOOSING INGREDIENTS

Many ingredients are naturally gluten-free. However, as a rule of thumb, you should avoid all baked goods (such as bread, biscuits, cakes, pastries, communion wafers and matzos), crisps, chips, pasta, pizza, stocks, soups, sauces (including soy sauce) and spices unless you know for sure they are gluten-free. You'll need to seek out specifically gluten-free versions of some products or check packaging to make sure the product doesn't contain gluten (some brands of baking powder, mustard or tomato ketchup contain added flour, for example, but others don't).

The above list of foods to avoid or check is only a guideline – always check the label for gluten-containing ingredients. In some cases, even naturally gluten-free foods are processed or packed in factories handling wheat and this can lead to trace gluten contamination – a problem for anyone who is highly sensitive. Contact the manufacturer if you're unsure.

There is no one product that will act as a direct replacement for wheat flour in every recipe. Gluten-free flours such as buckwheat flour, rice flour or gram flour all have their strengths and weaknesses. I tend to use brown rice flour because it is reasonably neutrally flavoured, has a similar level of carbohydrate to white wheat flour and contains various trace minerals and vitamins. However, rice flour doesn't absorb liquid as quickly as wheat flour so your dishes will often get a better texture if you leave the batter or dough to rest for 15 minutes or so.

Gluten-free flour blends are good for recipes that require a very neutral flavour (for instance, certain cakes and desserts). You can buy ready-prepared gluten-free flour blends that have been carefully formulated to mimic wheat flour as far as possible. I have based the recipes in this book on my own blend, but by all means use a commercial blend where a blend is required (it doesn't need to have added xanthan gum). If you would prefer to make your own, my recipe is on page 164. You may wonder why I use three different starches (tapioca flour, cornflour and potato flour) in my flour blend. The fact is that starch molecules from different sources behave in rather different ways and a mixture is often best.

AVOIDING CONTAMINATION

If you need to be truly gluten-free, then you will also need to ensure every item you use is scrupulously clean. If you have high gluten sensitivity and share your cooking equipment with others, don't use wooden utensils and chopping boards because the cracks may harbour gluten traces. Consider buying kitchen equipment for your exclusive use because it can be very difficult to clean certain items well enough to remove all traces of gluten. These are things such as (and this is not a complete list): toasters, waffle irons, sandwich toasters/panini presses, deep-fat fryers, sieves, wire racks, cake tins, baking beans and pastry brushes.

Bear in mind that butter, spreads, jams, honey, chutneys, mayonnaise and dips may also become contaminated by crumbs if shared with others.

INVALUABLE KITCHEN EQUIPMENT

Food processor: If you're eating a gluten-free diet, you'll almost certainly be doing a lot of cooking from scratch. A food processor will make this task a lot less labour-intensive. What I use most is the blending/mincing capability: it allows you to grind your own flours from nuts, purée soups and mince vegetables, among other things. If your budget doesn't stretch this far, at the very least I would recommend a hand-held blender with a food processor attachment. Buy the most powerful one you can afford.

Digital scales: The greater accuracy of digital scales compared with analogue, as well as the fact you can set the display back to zero (and thereby add your ingredients to the bowl as you go along), makes them a real help. Some offer liquid volume measurements as well, though be aware that this doesn't really work for oily or very sugary liquids because their density is different to watery ones.

Electric whisk: If you're not blessed with very muscular arms, then a hand-held electric whisk is a must. Whipping cream and whisking egg whites is extraordinarily tiring with a manual whisk! Some hand-held blenders come with a whisk attachment as a bonus.

CONVERTING RECIPES

As mentioned before, gluten is a complex protein. Gluten molecules love to link up with one another and when they do you get a stretchy gloop. Pour water into wheat flour and you'll get a somewhat gooey mixture that can be kneaded into an elastic dough. This stretchiness allows the dough to form wafer-thin layers – just think of filo pastry, the internal structure of fluffy bread or the laciness of crêpes.

However, wheat flour also has limitations and it's precisely because of this gluten content. Sometimes we don't want stretchy textures, for example in cakes or in shortcrust pastry. Some of the most common cooking practices are just a way to prevent gluten molecules meeting other gluten molecules. Creaming butter and sugar, then stirring in the flour means the gluten molecules become coated in fat, minimizing the chances of the gluten linking up and resulting in a lighter cake. Keeping shortcrust pastry cool also minimizes gluten linkage, giving a pleasantly crumbly pastry, not a tough one that is liable to shrink. Neither creaming nor keeping your mixture cool are necessary in gluten-free baking and, in fact, often you need to do the opposite to maximize the interactions within your dough. This may involve some kind of pre-cooking.

If you want to convert your own recipes, here are my top tips:

1 Take your time. If you just use rice flour or a flour blend as a direct substitute for wheat flour, with the same methods, you are likely to end up with gritty and crumbly bakes. For best results, whisk/blend everything really well, then leave your mixture to rest for a while. Add the raising agent (baking powder or bicarbonate of soda) mixed with a couple of teaspoons of water just before you transfer the mixture to the oven, or the raising agent will be activated too soon and your cake won't rise properly.

2 *Cut down on fat.* Generally speaking, gluten-free flours don't absorb fats and oils nearly as well as wheat flour does and if you're modifying an existing cake recipe this will mean you'll get an oily base. Reduce the butter/oil quantity by about one-fifth.

3 *Xanthan gum: less is more.* Xanthan gum is an additive that helps mimic some of the elastic qualities of gluten and will help to 'stick' your ingredients together. It will also minimize the gritty mouthfeel that can be associated with gluten-free baking. It is extremely useful for certain recipes, such as pastry or some breads. However, if you're not a fan of additives, there are many situations for which there is no need to use it, particularly if you have followed Tip 1, above. When you do use it, bear in mind that above a certain concentration it can make a mixture turn slimy – I often use just ¼ teaspoon per recipe.

Recipe Finder

SALADS, SOUPS & SNACKS

	Page	Contains no eggs	Contains no nuts	Dairy-free	Vegetarian	Vegan
Carrot & Apple Salad	16	•	•	•	•	•
Beetroot & Orange Salad	19	•	•	•	•	•
Warm Danish Potato Salad	20	•	•	•	•	
Thick Tomato Soup	23	•	•	•	•	•
Chicken Noodle Soup	24	•	•	•	•	
Leek & Potato Soup	25	•	•	•	•	
Minestrone	26	•	•	•	•	•
Seeded Buckwheat Rolls	29	•	•	•	•	
Chestnut & Pecan Loaf	30	•		•	•	•
Stovetop Italian Cornbread	31	•	•	•	•	
Garlic & Parmesan Flatbread	32	•	•	•	•	
Mini Onion Quiches with Mustard Pastry	35	•	•	•	•	
Onion Bhajis	36	•	•	•	•	•
Vegetable Samosas	38	•	•	•	•	•
Curried Lamb Pasties	39	•	•	•		
Kibbeh	40	•	•			
Simple Sushi	41	•	•	•	•	•
Prawns in Spicy Tempura	43	•	•	•	•	
Ham Croquetas	44	•	•	•		•

SAVOURY

	Page	Contains no eggs	Contains no nuts	Dairy-free	Vegetarian	Vegan
Asparagus, Spinach & Hollandaise Tart	48		•	•	•	
Roast Tomato, Rosemary & Goats' Cheese Tart	51	•	•		•	•
Pizza Margherita	52	•	•	•	•	•
Roast Vegetable Ratatouille	54	•	•	•	•	•
Mushroom & Gruyère Soufflé	55		•		•	•
Vegetable Cobbler	57	•	•	•	•	•
Squash & Spinach Curry	58	•	•	•	•	•
Battered Fish	60	•	•	•		
Smoked Salmon & Pesto Roulade	61	•	•	•		
Salmon with a Dill Crust	62	•	•	•	•	
Fish Pie	64	•	•	•		
Fish Fingers	65	•	•	•		
Chicken Kiev	67	•	•	•		
Chicken Paella	68	•	•	•	•	
Chicken Nuggets	71	•	•	•		
Coconut & Lime Chicken Curry	73	•	•	•		
Broccoli & Bacon Quiche	74	•	•			
Breaded Pork Escalopes	75	•	•	•		
Roast Pineapple & Mustard Ham	76	•	•	•		
Low-carb Lasagne	77	•	•		•	
Sweet & Sour Pork	78	•	•	•	•	
Leek & Pancetta Cannelloni	81	•	•		•	
Swedish Meatballs	82		•	•		
Chilli	84	•	•	•	•	
Beefburgers	87	•	•	•	•	•

Please note this is a guideline only; all ingredients should be checked for suitability before use.

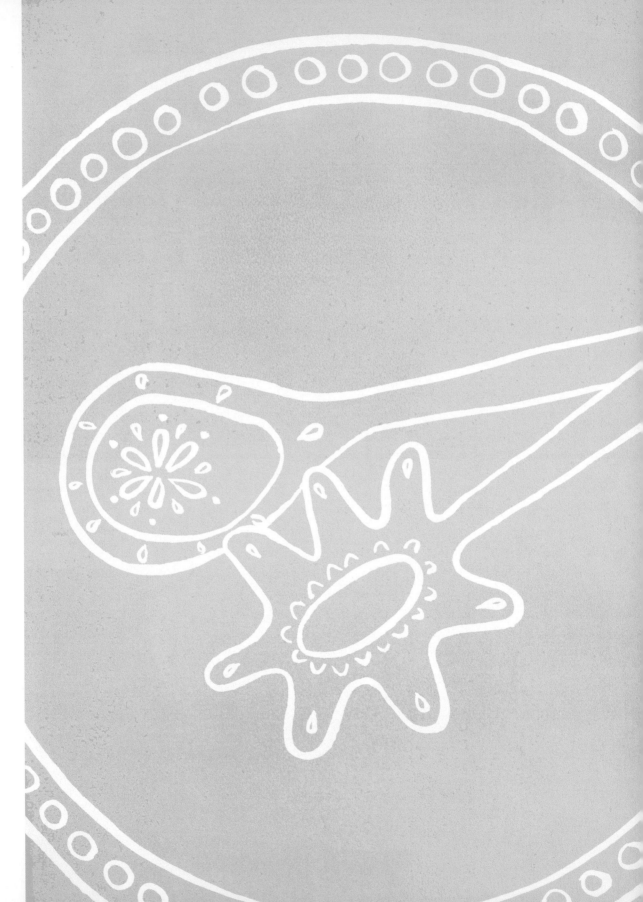

SALADS, SOUPS & SNACKS

2 large carrots, peeled and finely grated

4 small dessert apples, cored and coarsely grated

25g (1oz) granulated sugar

2 tablespoons boiling water

juice of 1 lemon

Place the grated carrots and apples in a serving bowl.

Put the sugar and measurement boiling water in a small cup and stir together until the sugar has dissolved. Add the lemon juice and mix together.

Pour the lemon mixture over the grated carrot and apple and stir until well combined. Chill for 30 minutes before serving.

Carrot & Apple Salad

This is a recipe from my mother and probably my favourite salad of all time (I do have a sweet tooth, though). The best part of it is the sweetened lemon dressing, which gives the salad a mouth-filling juiciness. I can eat a mountain of this; it's fantastic and my children beg me to make it, which I can say without understatement is unusual for a vegetable-based dish.

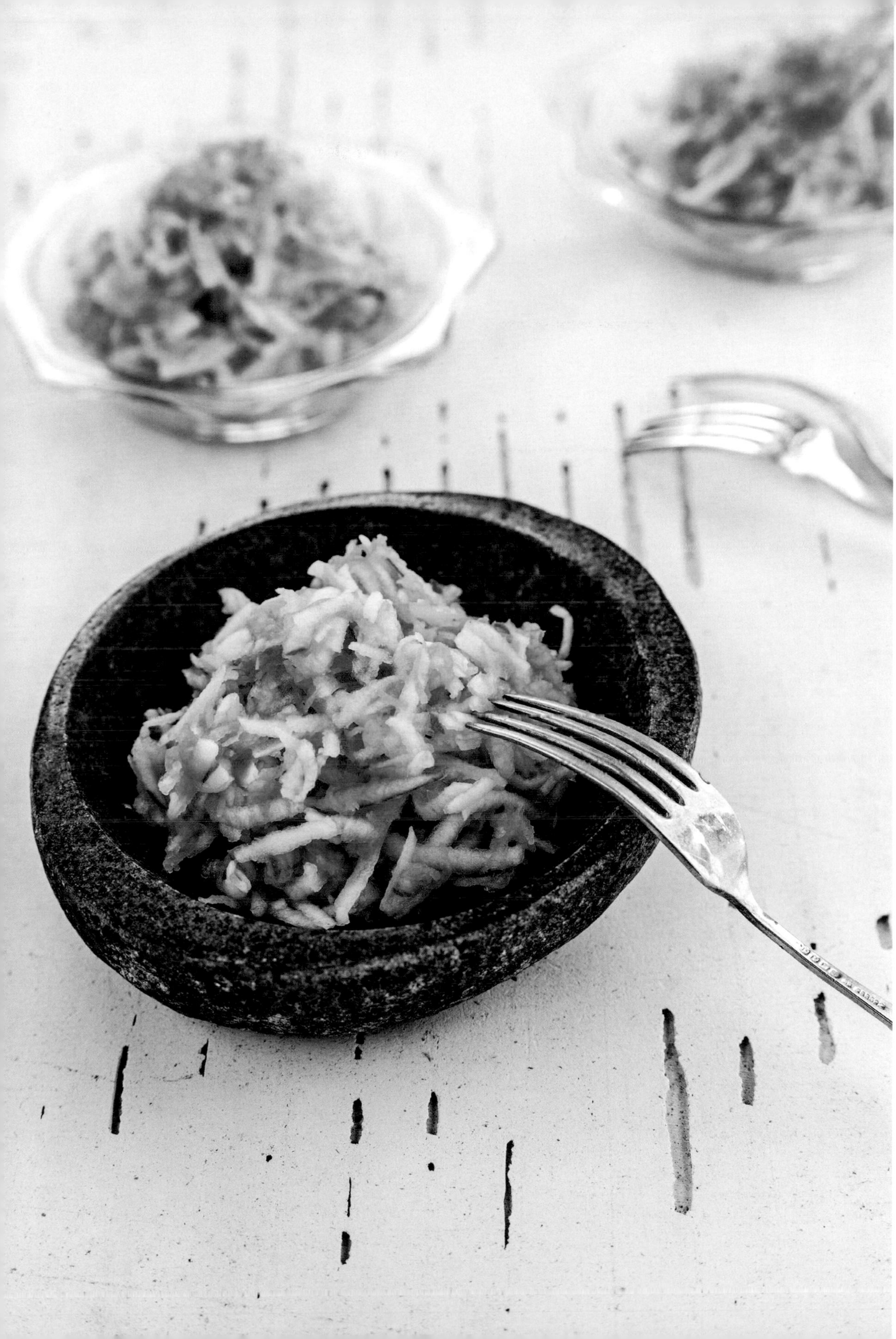

SERVES 3–4

3 small raw beetroot, about 175g (6oz) total weight, peeled, trimmed and cut into 5mm (¼ inch) slices

3 large oranges, such as navel

60g (2oz) rocket leaves

100g (3½oz) seedless grapes, each cut into 3 pieces

1 tablespoon lemon juice

1 tablespoon olive oil

pinch of salt

Cook the beetroot in a saucepan of boiling water for 10 minutes until tender, then drain and leave to cool. Cut each slice into quarters and place in a serving bowl.

Using a sharp knife, remove the peel and pith from the oranges, then cut out the segments, remove any seeds and chop into similar-sized pieces to the beetroot. Add the orange pieces, rocket and grapes to the beetroot.

Mix together the lemon juice, olive oil and salt in a cup, pour over the salad and toss together. Serve immediately.

Beetroot & Orange Salad

This is a refreshing yet simple salad with an attractive mix of colours. If you opt for ready-cooked beetroot, make sure it contains no vinegar, otherwise the flavour balance will be wrong.

500g (1lb) floury potatoes, peeled and cut into 5mm (¼ inch) thick slices

50g (2oz) unsalted butter

60ml (2fl oz) cider vinegar

2 teaspoons gluten-free mustard

2 onions, thinly sliced

salt and pepper

Cook the potatoes in a saucepan of boiling water for about 8–10 minutes until they are just starting to disintegrate. Drain, reserving 170ml (6fl oz) of the cooking water, then place the potatoes in a serving bowl.

Add the butter, vinegar and mustard to the reserved water in the pan, return to the heat and stir until the butter has melted. Add the onions and cook gently until almost soft but a hint of crunch remains – about 2–3 minutes.

Pour the onion mixture over the potatoes and carefully stir together to prevent the potatoes breaking up. Season with a little salt and pepper to taste. Serve immediately.

Warm Danish Potato Salad

This is the perfect salad for serving alongside sausages, especially the frankfurter kind. But it would also work as part of a vegetarian barbecued meal, with corn on the cob, griddled mushrooms and green salad.

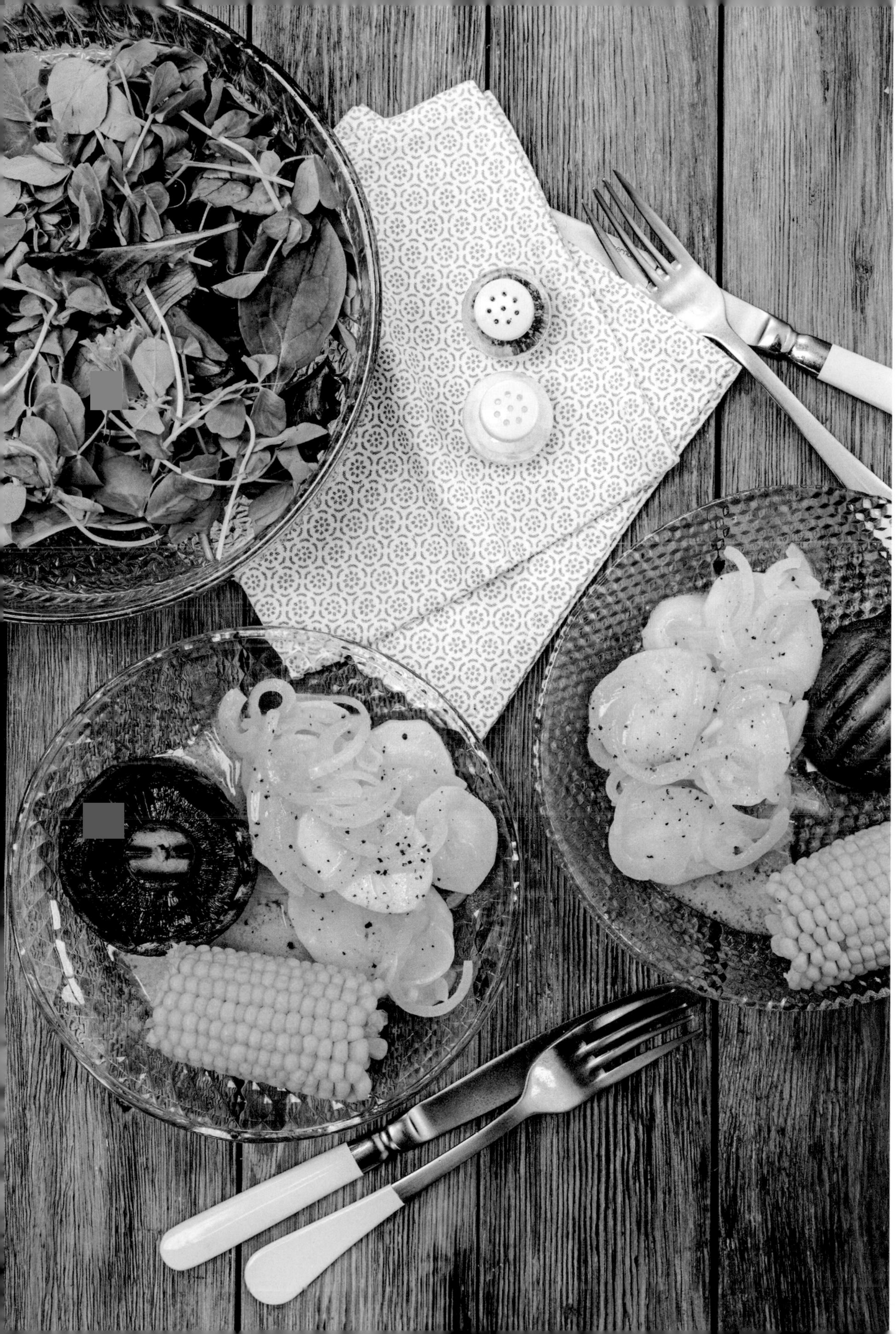

2 tablespoons olive oil

2 onions, sliced

4 garlic cloves, sliced

1.2kg (2½lb) ripe tomatoes, quartered

1 litre (1¾ pints) gluten-free vegetable stock

10 basil leaves

3 parsley sprigs

4 thyme sprigs

2 thick strips of grapefruit peel

2 tablespoons cornflour

125ml (4fl oz) single cream

granulated sugar, to taste

salt and pepper

Heat the oil in a large saucepan or flameproof casserole, add the onions and garlic and fry gently for about 5 minutes until soft but not brown. Add the tomatoes, stock, herbs and grapefruit peel and bring to the boil. Reduce the heat and simmer, uncovered, for 30 minutes until the tomatoes are completely soft.

Turn off the heat and leave the soup to stand for 10 minutes, then press through a sieve to remove the pips and skin. Pour the soup back into the casserole.

Mix together the cornflour and 4 tablespoons of the soup in a cup until smooth, then whisk into the soup and bring to the boil, whisking continuously. As soon as the soup bubbles, remove the pan from the heat and stir in the cream. Season to taste with salt and pepper, adding a little sugar if necessary, and serve.

Thick Tomato Soup

I'm a big fan of tomato soup from a can, but a few years ago I made my own – and it was fantastic! I particularly enjoy making a large batch of soup from my juicily ripe home-grown tomatoes, still warm from the sun, and freezing it to enjoy later in the year when the weather has turned cold.

2 carrots, peeled and cut into 3mm (⅛ inch) thick rounds

2 celery sticks, cut into 3mm (⅛ inch) thick rounds

1kg (2lb) chicken wings

2 bay leaves

2 teaspoons salt

½ teaspoon ground black pepper

2 litres (3½ pints) water

1 tablespoon chopped parsley

400g (13oz) gluten-free noodles, cut into 5cm (2 inch) lengths

Place the carrots, celery, chicken, bay leaves, salt, pepper and measurement water in a large stockpot. Bring to the boil, uncovered, then reduce the heat to medium-low and simmer for 3 hours, skimming off the fat with a spoon if necessary.

Leaving the pan on the heat, transfer the chicken pieces to a bowl using tongs, then remove the bay leaves and discard.

When the chicken is cool enough to handle, remove the skin and break off chunks of the meat. Return the meat to the soup, discarding the skin and bones.

Add the parsley, then bring the soup to the boil. Stir in the noodles and cook according to the packet instructions until tender. Serve hot.

Chicken Noodle Soup

This is a comforting soup for a cold day – or just because you have a cold! Though standard noodles are not suitable for gluten-free diets, this soup can be made with chopped-up rice vermicelli, gluten-free tagliatelle pasta or (my favourite) sweet potato vermicelli or cellophane noodles, also known as dang myun.

SERVES 4

4 teaspoons olive oil

4 large leeks, trimmed, cleaned and roughly sliced

500g (1lb) floury potatoes, peeled and roughly chopped

1.5 litres (2½ pints) water

4 parsley sprigs

2 thyme sprigs

2 bay leaves

125ml (4fl oz) single cream

salt and pepper

chopped chives, to serve

Heat the oil in a large saucepan or flameproof casserole, add the leeks and cook gently until softened but not brown. Add the potatoes, measurement water, herb sprigs and bay leaves and bring to the boil, then reduce the heat and simmer for about 30 minutes until the potatoes are tender. Remove the casserole from the heat and leave to stand for 15 minutes, then remove the herbs.

Using a hand-held blender or a food processor, blend the soup until smooth, then pass through a sieve and season to taste with salt and pepper.

To serve, return the soup to the casserole, add the cream and heat through until almost boiling. Serve sprinkled with chopped chives.

VARIATION
Use soya cream in place of the single cream to make a dairy-free version of this recipe.

Leek & Potato Soup

My most memorable bowl of leek and potato soup was in a French restaurant in Vietnam — the velvety smoothness and delicate flavour were so strikingly different to the local dishes I'd had. It seemed amazing that such variation could exist. The French call this soup vichyssoise and serve it cold, but personally I think it is a lot nicer served hot.

1 tablespoon olive oil

1 onion, diced

1 leek, trimmed, cleaned and cut into 1cm (½ inch) pieces

2 carrots, peeled and cut into 1cm (½ inch) pieces

2 celery sticks, cut into 1cm (½ inch) pieces

3 garlic cloves, finely chopped

2 rosemary sprigs, leaves chopped

handful of basil leaves, chopped

400g (13oz) can borlotti beans (or other bean of your choice), rinsed and drained

2 x 400g (13oz) cans chopped tomatoes

50g (2oz) risotto rice or short-grain pudding rice

1 litre (1¾ pints) gluten-free vegetable stock

1 white cabbage, halved, core removed and leaves roughly chopped

4 Savoy cabbage leaves, tough stalks removed and roughly chopped

salt and pepper

Heat the oil in a large saucepan or flameproof casserole, add the onion, leek, carrots, celery and garlic and stir well to coat in the oil. Cover with a lid and leave to cook gently for about 5 minutes.

Add the chopped herbs, beans, tomatoes, rice and stock, re-cover and cook for about 20 minutes.

Place the chopped cabbage on the surface of the soup, re-cover and cook for 5 minutes until just tender, then stir the leaves into the soup and cook for a further 5 minutes. Season to taste with salt and pepper and serve.

Minestrone

A bowlful of this soup has a kaleidoscope of colours and makes a great meal in itself. Though minestrone commonly contains pieces of pasta, here I've opted to use short-grain rice instead.

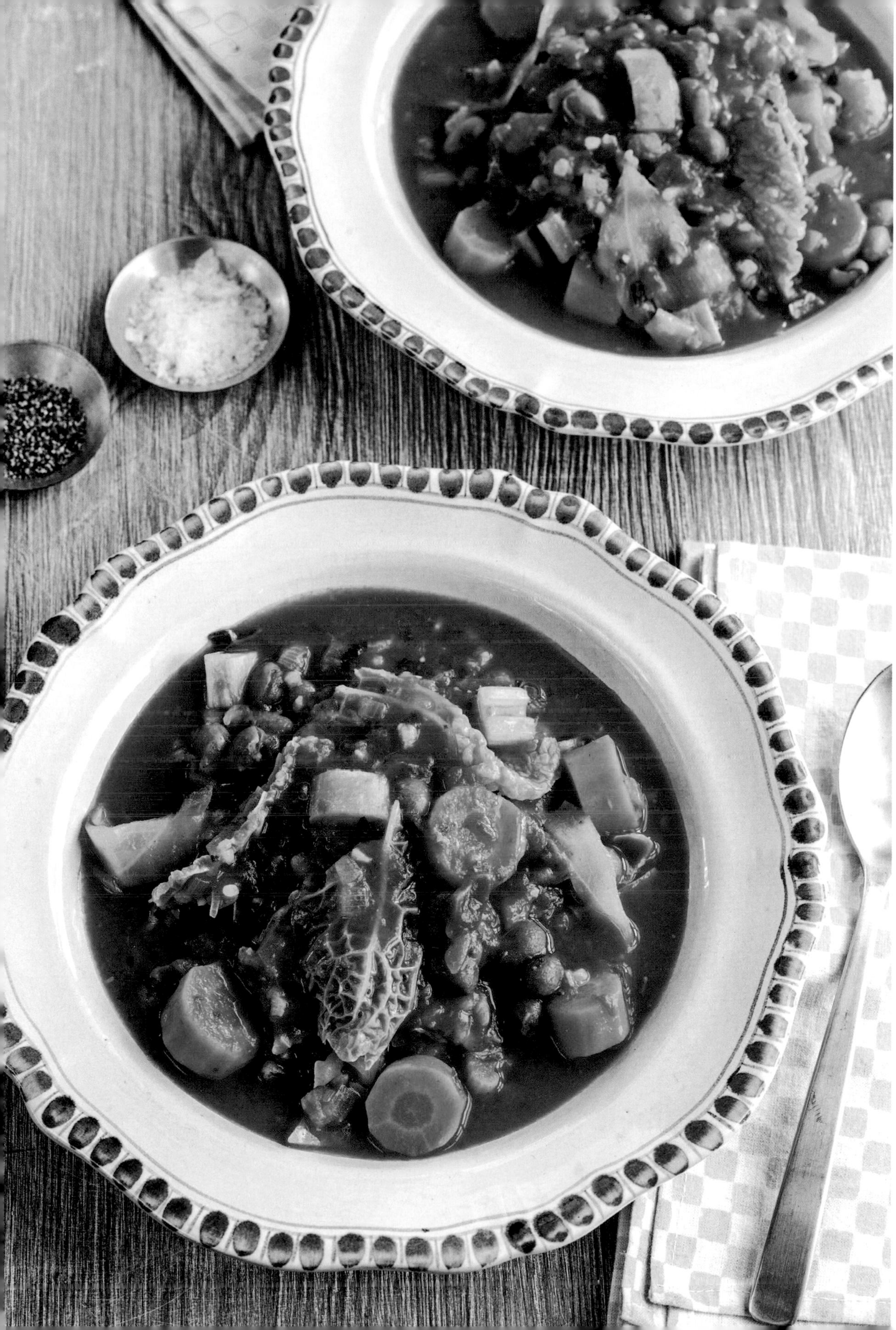

1 tablespoon sunflower oil, plus extra for greasing

60ml (2fl oz) hand-hot water

1 teaspoon fast-action dried yeast

1 teaspoon granulated sugar

50g (2oz) tapioca flour

125ml (4fl oz) milk, plus extra for brushing

150g (5oz) buckwheat flour, plus extra for dusting

¼ teaspoon salt

20g (¾oz) poppy seeds

20g (¾oz) sunflower seeds

VARIATION
Use soya milk in place of milk for a dairy-free version of this recipe.

Grease a large baking sheet with sunflower oil.

Stir together the warm water, yeast and sugar and set aside.

Place the tapioca flour, milk and oil in a saucepan over a medium-high heat and cook, stirring continuously, until it all clumps together in a sticky mass. Remove from the heat.

Place the buckwheat flour and salt in a large bowl. Stir in the yeasty liquid, then add the tapioca mixture. Using a spoon, turn the lump over until it is well coated in the flour. Using your hands, gradually knead in all the remaining flour: hold the lump of dough in both hands with your thumbs uppermost, then move your hands as if you are opening a book – this will gently stretch the top of the dough. Tuck the stretched dough underneath. The freshly exposed dough on top will be sticky, so dunk it in the flour. Repeat the stretching, tucking and dunking until there is no more loose flour left.

Turn the dough out on to a work surface well dusted with flour and continue to knead for a further 1 minute until well combined (keep your hands well floured). Reserving 2 teaspoons of the poppy seeds for sprinkling, knead the remaining seeds and the sunflower seeds into the dough.

Cut the dough into 4 equal-sized pieces and shape into round rolls. Place the rolls on the prepared baking sheet. Brush with a little milk and sprinkle over the reserved poppy seeds. Leave to rise in a warm place for about 1 hour or until doubled in size.

Preheat the oven to 160°C/325°F/Gas Mark 3. Bake for 25 minutes until browned and they sound hollow when you tap them. Leave to cool for a few minutes before serving.

Seeded Buckwheat Rolls

Deliciously crusty outside and spongy inside, these rolls are mainly made from buckwheat, a naturally gluten-free seed, but the key to success is the tapioca flour. When it is heated with liquid it becomes super-stretchy – perfect for bread.

150g (5oz) sweet potatoes, peeled and coarsely grated

300g (10oz) Gluten-free Plain White Flour Blend (see page 164)

250g (8oz) unsweetened chestnut purée

40g (1½oz) soft dark brown sugar

125ml (4fl oz) water

60ml (2fl oz) sunflower oil

3 eggs

½ teaspoon gluten-free ground nutmeg

pinch of salt

1½ teaspoons gluten-free baking powder

100g (3½oz) pecan nuts

20g (¾oz) linseeds

Preheat the oven to 150°C/300°F/Gas Mark 2. Line a 900g (2lb) loaf tin with nonstick baking paper.

Place the sweet potatoes, flour blend, chestnut purée, sugar, measurement water, oil, eggs, nutmeg and salt in a food processor and blend until well mixed. Leave to stand for 15 minutes (this improves the final texture).

Add the baking powder and pecans to the sweet potato mixture and blend for a few seconds, then stir in the linseeds. Pour into the prepared tin and smooth the top with a spatula.

Bake for 60–70 minutes until the edges of the loaf are pulling away from the tin and a skewer inserted in the centre comes out clean. Transfer the loaf to a wire rack and leave to cool.

Chestnut & Pecan Loaf

This moist and nutritious high-fibre loaf is lovely thickly sliced and served with cheese, or spread with butter as an accompaniment to soup. It will keep for a couple of days in an airtight tin.

2 tablespoons olive oil

1 red onion, sliced

2 teaspoons chopped rosemary

125ml (4fl oz) milk

1 teaspoon balsamic vinegar

1 egg

1 tablespoon tomato purée

150g (5oz) cornmeal

½ teaspoon bicarbonate of soda

½ teaspoon salt

Heat half the oil in a 20cm (8 inch) nonstick frying pan over a hob ring about the same diameter as the pan. Add the onion and rosemary and cook over a medium heat for about 2–3 minutes until the onion is slightly translucent.

Meanwhile, put the milk, vinegar, egg, tomato purée and remaining oil in a small bowl or jug and mix together. In a separate bowl, stir together the cornmeal, bicarbonate of soda and salt. Quickly pour the wet ingredients into the dry ingredients and stir well, then pour into the frying pan, level with a spatuala and cover with a lid.

Reduce the heat to low and cook for 8–10 minutes. The steam will help to cook the bread and it's done when the centre becomes solid – the surface should look dry and a skewer inserted into the centre should come out clean. Remove the pan from the heat and keep covered. To serve, invert on to a plate.

VARIATION
Use soya milk in place of the milk to create a dairy-free version of this recipe.

Stovetop Italian Cornbread

This bread is a cross between an American cornbread and an Italian focaccia. It is best eaten warm, and you can easily whip it up just before a meal. Because no oven is needed, this is a brilliant recipe for a camping trip, too.

SERVES 4

25g (1oz) salted butter, softened, plus extra for greasing

125g (4oz) tapioca flour

60ml (2fl oz) boiling water

60ml (2fl oz) olive oil

75g (3oz) Parmesan or other hard cheese, finely grated

1 egg, lightly beaten

1 garlic clove, crushed

2 teaspoons chopped parsley

Preheat the oven to 180°C/350°F/Gas Mark 4. Lightly grease a baking sheet with butter.

Place the tapioca flour in a heatproof bowl. Pour over the measurement boiling water and stir vigorously (there will still be quite a lot of dry flour, but this is normal). Stir in the oil and grated cheese, then add the egg and stir thoroughly to create a sticky dough.

Spoon the dough out on to the prepared baking sheet, then using a spatula, pat it into a large oval about 1cm (½ inch) thick. Bake for 20 minutes until puffed up and browned.

Meanwhile, place the garlic and butter in a bowl and mix together, then mix in the parsley. Remove the flatbread from the oven and smear it with the butter. Return to the oven and bake for a further 10 minutes. Serve hot.

Garlic & Parmesan Flatbread

Cheese and a top smothered with garlic butter raises this flatbread above an everyday offering. Perfect for tearing and sharing, it's based on Brazil's pão de queijo, but with an Italian twist.

1 tablespoon olive oil

2 onions, thinly sliced

2 eggs

2 teaspoons thyme leaves,
plus extra sprigs to garnish

Pastry

75g (3oz) cold unsalted butter,
diced, plus extra for greasing

100g (3½oz) brown rice flour,
plus extra for dusting

75g (3oz) gram (chickpea) flour

½ teaspoon xanthan gum

4 teaspoons gluten-free
wholegrain mustard

1 tablespoon water

Preheat the oven to 180°C/350°F/Gas Mark 4. Grease the sections of a 12-hole tart tin with butter.

To make the pastry, place the rice flour, gram flour and xanthan gum in a bowl. Add the butter and rub in with the fingertips until the mixture resembles breadcrumbs. Stir in the mustard, then add the measurement water. Using your hands, combine well to form a soft but not sticky dough, adding a little more water or rice flour if necessary. Wrap in clingfilm and chill for 30 minutes.

Roll out the pastry to about 3mm (⅛ inch) thick on a work surface dusted with rice flour. Stamp out 12 rounds using a pastry cutter a little larger than the tin sections. Alternatively, use a jar lid to cut round. Press the pastry rounds into the tin sections. (Don't worry too much about perfection, but if there are cracks or holes use a little of the excess pastry to fix them.) Bake for 10 minutes, then leave to cool in the tin.

To make the filling, heat the oil in a nonstick frying pan, add the onions and cook over a medium heat for about 5–10 minutes until softened and starting to turn brown.

Beat together the eggs in a jug, then add the thyme leaves. Stir in the warm onions, then use a fork to transfer the mixture evenly into the pastry cases.

Bake for 10 minutes until the filling has set. Carefully remove the quiches from the tin, then serve warm or cold, garnished with thyme sprigs.

Mini Onion Quiches with Mustard Pastry

A nutritious alternative to wheat flour, gram flour is particularly good in savoury dishes. Here the mustard marries well with the sweetness of the onions and earthiness of the thyme. Try these little quiches for a picnic, in a lunchbox or as a party snack.

2 onions

1 tablespoon olive oil, plus extra for greasing

75g (3oz) gram (chickpea) flour

½ teaspoon gluten-free ground turmeric

¼ teaspoon gluten-free ground coriander

¼ teaspoon gluten-free ground cumin

pinch of salt

2 tablespoons water

1 tablespoon mango chutney

1 teaspoon tomato purée

Preheat the oven to 180°C/350°F/Gas Mark 4.

Cut the onions in half, top to bottom, then slice each half into 3–4mm (⅛–¼ inch) slices. Heat the oil in a nonstick frying pan, add the onion slices and fry gently for about 5 minutes until soft but not brown.

Place the gram flour, spices and salt in a bowl and add the fried onions. Add the measurement water, chutney and tomato purée and stir together until the mixture is smooth but not sloppy – it should be moist enough to make stirring easy.

Drizzle a lipped baking sheet with oil, then place 8 dollops of the onion mixture on to the sheet using tablespoons. You might need to flatten the heaps a little with the back of a spoon.

Bake for 15 minutes, then remove the sheet from the oven and gently move it from side to side to redistribute the oil. Using a fish slice, flip the bhajis over, then return to the oven and bake for a further 15 minutes until well browned and glistening.

Onion Bhajis

Onion bhajis are one of my favourite snack foods, but until I tried to make them I didn't realize they could be so easy. I don't have a deep-fat fryer, so this version can be done on a baking sheet in the oven. Eat these the same day, hot or cold, and serve with mango chutney or a dip made of natural or soya yogurt and chopped fresh mint.

MAKES 12

2 teaspoons olive oil

1 small onion, finely diced

2 teaspoons gluten-free curry powder

50g (2oz) peeled potatoes, finely diced

1 small carrot, finely diced

2 teaspoons tomato purée

1 teaspoon mango chutney

125ml (4fl oz) water

25g (1oz) frozen peas

½ teaspoon salt

1 tablespoon chopped fresh coriander

sunflower oil, for shallow-frying

Pastry

150g (5oz) Gluten-free Plain White Flour Blend (see page 164)

100g (3½oz) gram (chickpea) flour, plus extra for dusting

125ml (4fl oz) water

2 tablespoons olive oil

½ teaspoon xanthan gum

1 teaspoon poppy seeds

pinch of salt

To make the pastry, place all the ingredients in a bowl and combine to form a soft but not sticky dough, adding a little more water if necessary. Wrap in clingfilm and place in the refrigerator to chill.

Heat the olive oil in a heavy-based saucepan, add the onion and fry gently for about 3–4 minutes until softened. Add the curry powder and cook for a further 10 seconds, then stir in the potatoes, carrot, tomato purée, chutney and measurement water. Cover with a lid, reduce the heat to low and simmer for 5 minutes until the vegetables are just tender. Add the peas, salt and coriander, then remove the pan from the heat and set aside.

To make the samosas, roll out the dough to about 3mm (⅛ inch) thick on a work surface dusted with gram flour. Using a 15cm (6 inch) diameter bowl or side plate as a template, cut out 6 pastry rounds, then cut each round in half. Wet the curved edges with a little water and fold over the semi-circles to form rough triangle shapes, pinching the curved edges shut to form cones of pastry. Spoon 2 teaspoons of the filling into each pastry cone and seal the remaining edges by dabbing with a little water and pinching shut.

Arrange 4 samosas in a circle in a deep frying pan or saucepan. Pour in sunflower oil to the depth of about 1cm (½ inch) and heat over a medium-high heat. Fry the samosas for about 1–2 minutes until golden brown, then flip them over using a slotted spoon and fry for a further 1–2 minutes. Remove from the pan with a slotted spoon, drain on kitchen paper and keep warm in a low oven while you cook the remaining samosas.

Vegetable Samosas

Forget the shop-bought flaccid triangles that masquerade as samosas – these homemade ones are delicately crispy and golden brown. Cut the vegetables into tiny chunks, otherwise the samosas will break open. Eat within a couple of days.

2 teaspoons olive oil,
plus extra for greasing

4 teaspoons gluten-free curry
powder

1 quantity gluten-free Plain
Shortcrust Pastry (see page 166)

100g (3½oz) minced lamb

1 small onion, finely chopped

1 garlic clove, finely chopped

½ teaspoon cayenne pepper

¼ teaspoon gluten-free
ground cinnamon

¼ teaspoon gluten-free
ground ginger

¼ teaspoon ground black pepper

¼ teaspoon salt

2 teaspoons tomato purée

30g (1oz) frozen peas

60ml (2fl oz) water

cornflour, for dusting

Preheat the oven to 180°C/350°F/Gas Mark 4. Lightly grease
a baking sheet with oil.

Knead half the curry powder into the pastry, then wrap
in clingfilm and chill while you make the filling.

Heat the oil in a saucepan, add the lamb and fry over
a medium heat for about 10 minutes, breaking it up with
a wooden spoon, until browned and cooked through. Drain
off any liquid and transfer the lamb to a bowl. Set aside.

Add the onion and garlic to the pan with the remaining
curry powder, cayenne, cinnamon, ginger, pepper and salt
and fry gently for about 5 minutes until the onion is softened.
Add the lamb, tomato purée, peas and measurement water
and cook for a further 5 minutes, then remove from the heat.

Roll out the pastry to about 4mm (¼ inch) thick on a work
surface dusted with cornflour (if the pastry starts to crack,
knead in a drop of water). Stamp out about 12 rounds using
a 9cm (3½ inch) diameter pastry cutter. Alternatively, use
a jar lid to cut round.

Place 1 heaped teaspoon of the filling on the lower half of
a pastry round, then lightly wet the edge with water. Fold
over the top half of the pastry and press the edges together
to seal. Using your fingertip, form a frilled edge (if the
pastry starts to crack, brush with a little water). Repeat
with the remaining pastry rounds and filling.

Place the pasties on the prepared baking sheet and bake
for 25 minutes until golden. Serve warm or cold.

Curried Lamb Pasties

For a time I lived in Brixton, London, where I discovered the
delights of Caribbean cookery. These little pasties are inspired
by traditional Jamaican patties, with their spicy lamb filling and
curried pastry, and are great for lunchboxes, picnics or parties.

250ml (8fl oz) water

80g (3oz) quinoa, rinsed and drained

30g (1oz) pine nuts

500g (1lb) lean minced lamb

1 small onion

4 teaspoons cornflour

4 teaspoons redcurrant jelly

4 teaspoons chopped rosemary

1 teaspoon gluten-free ground cinnamon

1 teaspoon salt

½ teaspoon ground black pepper

olive oil, for drizzling

Preheat the oven to 160°C/325°F/Gas Mark 3.

Pour the measurement water into a saucepan and bring to the boil, then add the quinoa and simmer for 15 minutes, or according to the packet instructions. Remove the pan from the heat and leave to stand until all the liquid has been absorbed.

Meanwhile, toast the pine nuts in a dry frying pan until lightly browned.

Place the lamb, onion, cornflour, redcurrant jelly, rosemary, cinnamon, salt and pepper in a food processor. Add the toasted pine nuts and blend to a thick paste. Stir in the quinoa.

Divide the mixture into 12–15 equal-sized balls and form into egg-shaped patties. Place on a baking sheet and drizzle with olive oil. Shake the tray to coat the kibbeh in the oil.

Bake for 15 minutes, then remove from the oven and gently move the kibbeh around on the sheet. Increase the oven temperature to 180°C/350°F/Gas Mark 4 and return the kibbeh to the oven for a further 15 minutes until nicely browned and cooked through – cut the largest kibbeh in half to check the meat is cooked; if not, cook them a little longer.

Kibbeh

Kibbeh are meat snacks from the Middle East, traditionally made using bulgar wheat, which contains gluten. This simple version uses quinoa instead.

200g (7oz) sushi rice

500ml (17fl oz) water

2 teaspoons rice vinegar

½ ripe avocado

1 carrot, peeled

½ yellow pepper, cored
and deseeded

¼ cucumber, deseeded

2 sheets of sushi nori
(dark seaweed sheets)

Place the rice in a heavy-based saucepan, add the measurement water and bring to the boil. Cover with a lid, then cook over a medium heat for about 15 minutes until the rice is tender and the liquid has been absorbed. Leave to cool, then gently mix in the rice vinegar.

When ready to assemble, stone and peel the avocado, then dice into 3mm (⅛ inch) cubes along with the carrot, yellow pepper and cucumber.

Place your first sheet of sushi nori, shiny side down, on a sushi mat or clean tea towel, aligning it with the bottom edge. Spread half the rice evenly across the sheet, leaving a 1cm (½ inch) strip at the top uncovered. Lay half the vegetables over the width of the rice, leaving about 2cm (¾ inch) of rice uncovered at the top and bottom.

Starting at the bottom of the sheet, apply an even, gentle pressure while you roll it up to form a tight sausage of sushi, using the mat or tea towel to help you. Lightly wet the top strip and press to form a seal. Using a sharp knife (it can help to wet the blade a little), cut the roll into 10 slices. Repeat with the remaining ingredients.

Simple Sushi

Though sushi is most commonly associated with fish, there are actually lots of possible vegetable fillings and it is also really easy to make. Don't be put off if you lack a sushi mat because a clean tea towel works just as well. Serve with tiny bowls of gluten-free tamari, wasabi paste and sushi ginger. Eat the same day.

SERVES 4

300g (10oz) cooked peeled
prawns, rinsed and drained

50g (2oz) brown rice flour

60ml (2fl oz) water

2 teaspoons chopped chives

1 teaspoon gluten-free
ground ginger

4 teaspoons chilli oil

pinch of salt

2 egg whites

sunflower oil, for shallow-frying

sweet chilli sauce or garlic
mayonnaise, to serve

Pat the prawns dry using kitchen paper and set aside.

To make the batter, stir together the rice flour, measurement
water, chives, ginger, chilli oil and salt in a bowl. In a separate,
thoroughly clean bowl, whisk the egg whites until frothy,
stopping before they get to the soft-peak stage. Add the
rice mixture and whisk until combined. Stir the prawns
into the batter.

Pour sunflower oil into a wok or large saucepan to the depth
of about 1cm (½ inch) and heat to 170°C (340°F), or until
a drop of batter sizzles gently in the oil.

Using tongs or chopsticks, gently drop about 8 prawns into
the hot oil and fry for about 1 minute until golden, then flip
over and cook for a further 1–2 minutes until golden-brown
all over. (The prawns should bubble gently with a constant
sound of gentle sizzling and without violent spitting.) Remove
with a slotted spoon and drain on kitchen paper. Repeat until
all the prawns are cooked. Serve immediately with sweet
chilli sauce or garlic mayonnaise.

Prawns in Spicy Tempura

Tempura batter is a Japanese speciality and making it with rice
flour works really well. This recipe uses prawns, but strips of carrot,
courgette or red pepper are also delicious. Most conventional
recipes stress the need for ice-cold water, but that is not necessary
for this gluten-free version. Use the batter as soon as it is made.

MAKES ABOUT 10

50g (2oz) butter

80g (3oz) cornflour

250ml (8fl oz) gluten-free
vegetable stock

25g (1oz) ham, finely diced

¼ teaspoon salt

¼ teaspoon ground black pepper

50g (2oz) instant cornmeal

sunflower oil, for shallow-frying

Melt the butter in a heavy-based saucepan, then stir in the cornflour and whisk until lump-free. Gradually add the stock, whisking until smooth. Bring to the boil and cook for about 2 minutes, stirring continuously, until thick. Stir in the ham, salt and pepper, then leave to cool completely (the mixture will then be very firm and easy to mould).

Tip the cornmeal into a bowl. Take 1 tablespoon of the ham mixture and shape it into a cylinder about the length of your index finger. Roll it in the cornmeal until well coated, then transfer to a plate. Repeat until all the ham mixture is used up – it makes about 10 croquetas.

Pour sunflower oil into a heavy-based saucepan to the depth of about 1cm (½ inch) and heat to 180°C (350°F), or until a small cube of gluten-free bread sizzles in the oil. Using a slotted spoon, lower the croquetas into the hot oil and fry for 2 minutes on each side (they won't go brown). Remove with a slotted spoon and drain on crumpled kitchen paper. Serve hot.

VARIATION
Use 25g (1oz) finely chopped cooked mushrooms in place of the ham for a vegetarian version.

Ham Croquetas

Often served as a tapas dish, ham croquetas, or croquettes, are defined by a creamy interior and crisp exterior. These croquetas are made in the traditional way – with a filling made from Béchamel sauce, rather than potato – while the crunchy coating is simply a layer of cornmeal.

SAVOURY

SERVES 4–6

250g (8oz) fresh asparagus, trimmed and cut into 2cm (¾ inch) pieces

1 quantity gluten-free Plain Shortcrust Pastry (see page 166)

Spinach filling

150g (5oz) spinach leaves, tough stalks removed

100g (3½oz) ricotta cheese

2 teaspoons garlic purée

1 egg

Hollandaise filling

20g (¾oz) cornflour, plus extra for dusting

100g (3½oz) unsalted butter

150g (5oz) ricotta cheese

2 eggs

juice of ½ lemon

¼ teaspoon salt

Preheat the oven to 180°C/350°F/Gas Mark 4.

Cook the asparagus in a saucepan of boiling water for about 8 minutes until very tender, then drain.

Meanwhile, roll out the pastry to about 4mm (¼ inch) thick on a work surface well dusted with cornflour. Line a 20cm (8 inch) tart tin with the pastry and trim any excess using a sharp knife.

To make the spinach filling, steam the spinach for about 1 minute until it wilts, then squeeze out any moisture. Blend the spinach, ricotta, garlic purée and egg in a food processor or blender until smooth.

Scatter the asparagus over the pastry case, then pour in the spinach mixture.

To make the Hollandaise filling, melt the butter in a saucepan, then stir in the cornflour and whisk until smooth. Add the ricotta, eggs, lemon juice and salt and whisk until combined. Spoon the mixture evenly over the spinach in the pastry case.

Bake for 30 minutes until the filling is set and has started to brown slightly.

Asparagus, Spinach & Hollandaise Tart

Buttery soft asparagus is mixed with spinach in a lemony Hollandaise-style filling, while the combination of dark green and pale yellow make this vegetarian tart particularly attractive. This tart can be enjoyed hot or cold.

SERVES 4–6

250g (8oz) cherry tomatoes

2 finger-length rosemary sprigs

2 teaspoons olive oil

1 quantity gluten-free Plain Shortcrust Pastry (see page 166)

cornflour, for dusting

100g (3½oz) soft goats' cheese, such as chèvre blanc, cut into small pieces

3 eggs

60ml (2fl oz) milk

salt and pepper

Preheat the oven to 120°C/250°F/Gas Mark ½.

Wash and dry the tomatoes, then place in a small roasting tin with the leaves from the rosemary and the olive oil. Toss the tomatoes to coat them in the oil, then bake for 30 minutes.

Meanwhile, roll out the pastry to about 4mm (¼ inch) thick on a work surface well dusted with cornflour. Line a 20cm (8 inch) tart tin with the pastry and trim any excess using a sharp knife. Scatter the goats' cheese evenly over the pastry case.

Beat together the eggs, milk and a little salt and pepper in a small bowl.

Tip the roasted tomatoes, rosemary and oil into the pastry case and spread out evenly across the case. Pour over the egg mixture.

Increase the oven temperature to 180°C/350°F/Gas Mark 4 and bake the tart for 30 minutes until golden and the filling is set.

Roast Tomato, Rosemary & Goats' Cheese Tart

This tart was a favourite of mine after I left university and it has been an easy meal option ever since. I love it with a fresh green salad and boiled new potatoes.

2 teaspoons olive oil

1 small onion, roughly chopped

2 garlic cloves, roughly chopped

400g (13oz) can chopped tomatoes

2 tablespoons tomato purée

¼ teaspoon salt

250g (8oz) grated mozzarella cheese

basil leaves, to garnish

Dough

100g (3½oz) tapioca flour

250ml (8fl oz) milk

2½ teaspoons fast-action dried yeast

2 teaspoons granulated sugar

60ml (2fl oz) hand-hot water

225g (7½oz) Gluten-free Plain White Flour Blend (see page 164), plus extra for dusting

2 tablespoons olive oil, plus extra for greasing

1 tablespoon dried milk

½ teaspoon salt

cornmeal, for dusting

To make the dough, place the tapioca flour and milk in a saucepan and heat, stirring occasionally, until it comes together as a very stretchy white lump. Remove the pan from the heat.

Stir together the yeast, sugar and warm water in a cup. Place 150g (5oz) of the flour blend in a large bowl and add the oil, dried milk and salt. Add the tapioca mixture to the bowl and, using a spoon, turn the lump over until it is well coated in flour.

Pour in the yeasty liquid and knead together until a dough forms, then turn it out on to a work surface lightly dusted with flour blend and continue to knead for 1 minute. Put it back in the bowl, cover with oiled clingfilm and leave in a warm place for about 1 hour until doubled in size. Knead in the remaining flour blend, then leave to rise for a further 30 minutes.

Meanwhile, heat the oil in a saucepan, add the onion and garlic and fry gently for about 5 minutes until softened, then add the tomatoes, tomato purée and salt. Simmer for 4 minutes until the sauce is reduced, then leave to cool slightly. Using a hand-held blender or food processor, blend the sauce until smooth.

Preheat the oven to 180°C/350°F/Gas Mark 4. If you have a pizza stone, pop it in the oven; if not, preheat a baking sheet.

Turn the dough out on to a work surface dusted with flour blend and cornmeal. Divide the dough into 4 equal-sized pieces and shape into thick rounds. Place 1 round on the preheated pizza stone or baking sheet and use your fingers to carefully spread out the dough until it is about 5mm (¼ inch) thick. Spread a layer of tomato sauce on top and sprinkle with a quarter of the mozzarella. Repeat with the remaining dough to make 4 pizzas.

Bake for 15 minutes until golden and the cheese has melted. Serve immediately, topped with basil leaves.

Pizza Margherita

This recipe will make four cheese and tomato pizzas with light, airy bases – what you choose to add to them is up to you! Cooked tapioca flour gives all-important stretchiness to the dough, while cornmeal adds a touch of authenticity and crunch.

2 onions, roughly chopped

1 red pepper, cored, deseeded and roughly chopped

1 green pepper, cored, deseeded and roughly chopped

2 courgettes, roughly chopped

250g (8oz) cherry tomatoes, halved

3 garlic cloves, thinly sliced

60ml (2fl oz) olive oil

1 oregano sprig

2 thyme sprigs

1 aubergine, cut into 2cm (¾ inch) cubes

4 teaspoons tomato purée

salt and pepper

Preheat the oven to 180°C/350°F/Gas Mark 4.

Place the onions, peppers, courgettes, tomatoes and garlic in a roasting tin, add the oil, oregano and thyme and toss together. Roast for 20 minutes until just tender.

Place the aubergine and tomato purée in a large saucepan, scrape in the roasted vegetables, including the oil, and stir well.

Cook over a medium heat for 20 minutes until all the vegetables are tender. Season to taste with salt and pepper and serve.

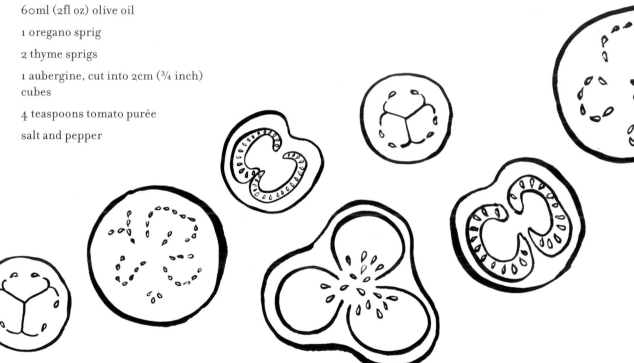

Roast Vegetable Ratatouille

Ratatouille is a jewel-coloured Provençal dish that uses tomatoes, aubergine, peppers and courgettes. It is typically cooked on the stovetop, but in this version I start off the process in the oven for a slightly sweeter taste. I like to serve this ratatouille with fish or gluten-free pasta, in particular.

SERVES 4

25g (1oz) unsalted butter,
plus extra for greasing

1 teaspoon olive oil

250g (8oz) mushrooms,
finely diced

40g (1½oz) cornflour

170ml (6fl oz) gluten-free
vegetable stock

80g (3oz) Gruyère cheese, grated

2 teaspoons gluten-free
wholegrain mustard

3 eggs, separated

Preheat the oven to 180°C/350°F/Gas Mark 4. Grease a deep 850ml (1½ pint) ovenproof dish with butter.

Heat the oil in a nonstick frying pan, add the mushrooms and fry gently for about 5 minutes until golden. Set aside.

Melt the butter in a saucepan, then stir in the cornflour and whisk until it forms a lump-free paste. Gradually add the vegetable stock, stirring continuously until the sauce is thickened. Remove the pan from the heat and stir in the grated cheese and mustard. Leave to cool for 10 minutes.

Whisk the egg whites in a thoroughly clean bowl until stiff. Stir the egg yolks and mushrooms into the cheese sauce, then carefully fold in the whites. Pour the mixture into the prepared dish and bake for 45 minutes until puffy and golden brown.

Mushroom & Gruyère Soufflé

This soufflé is great on its own as a starter, or served with new potatoes and green vegetables as a main. Don't be put off by any stories you may have heard about soufflés being temperamental: I've been cooking them since I was about 12 years old and have never had a problem. You don't even need to be too worried about the exact cooking time: by turning the heat down to about 100°C/225°F/Gas Mark ¼ you can keep your soufflé quite happy for 10–15 minutes until needed (just don't open the oven door until the last minute or your masterpiece may collapse).

1 tablespoon olive oil

1 onion, diced

2 leeks, trimmed, cleaned and finely sliced

2 celery sticks, finely sliced

2 carrots, peeled and cut into 1cm (½ inch) cubes

2 small parsnips, peeled and cut into 1cm (½ inch) cubes

2 courgettes, cut into 1cm (½ inch) cubes

1 red pepper, cored, deseeded and sliced

1 yellow pepper, cored, deseeded and sliced

5 closed cup mushrooms, sliced

400g (13oz) can gluten-free baked beans

salt

Dumplings

100g (3½oz) pure vegetable fat, chilled in the freezer

150g (5oz) gram (chickpea) flour

40g (1½oz) cornflour

1 teaspoon gluten-free baking powder

handful of parsley, chopped

pinch of salt

60ml (2fl oz) water

Heat the oil in a large flameproof casserole, add the onion, leeks and celery and cook over a medium heat for about 5 minutes until softened. Add the remaining vegetables to the casserole and cook for a further 5–10 minutes until soft.

Add the baked beans, then half-fill the empty can with water and add to the pan. Cover with a lid and bring to the boil, then reduce the heat and simmer for 1½ hours. Season to taste with salt.

Towards the end of the cooking time, preheat the oven to 160°C/325°F/Gas Mark 3. To make the dumplings, grate the frozen vegetable fat into a bowl. Stir in the gram flour, cornflour, baking powder, parsley and salt, then add the measurement water and knead to a soft but not sticky dough, adding a little more water if necessary. Divide the dough into 8 equal-sized pieces and shape into balls, then drop them into the stew.

Transfer the casserole to the oven, uncovered, and cook for about 35 minutes until the dumplings have browned on top. Serve immediately.

Vegetable Cobbler

This vegetable stew formed more or less my staple diet at university. I serve it here with dumplings, which bake in the stew while it cooks in the oven, and end up with crispy tops and fluffy middles.

500g (1lb) butternut squash, peeled, deseeded and cut into 1cm (½ inch) cubes

60ml (2fl oz) olive oil

4 green cardamoms

2 teaspoons cumin seeds

10 whole cloves

2 onions, finely chopped

4 garlic cloves, finely chopped

thumb-sized piece of fresh root ginger, peeled and finely grated

2 teaspoons ground black pepper

4 teaspoons gluten-free curry powder

1 teaspoon granulated sugar

500ml (17fl oz) passata

2 x 400g (13oz) cans chickpeas, rinsed and drained

200g (7oz) spinach leaves, tough stalks removed and torn into pieces

salt

Preheat the oven to 180°C/350°F/Gas Mark 4.

Place the squash in a roasting tin and toss together with half the olive oil until evenly coated. Bake for 45 minutes until golden brown and tender.

Meanwhile, remove the seeds from the cardamom pods and place in a pestle and mortar or spice grinder with the cumin seeds and cloves. Grind to a fine powder.

Heat the remaining oil in a large heavy-based saucepan over a medium-high heat, add the onions and fry gently for about 5 minutes until softened. Add the garlic, ginger, pepper, curry powder and ground spices and cook for a few minutes.

Stir in the sugar, passata and chickpeas. Fill 1 empty chickpea can with water and add to the pan, then reduce the heat and simmer for 20 minutes. Stir in the cooked squash and simmer for a further 10 minutes.

Place the spinach on top of the curry, but don't stir in – leave for a few minutes until the leaves wilt, then stir them in and season to taste with salt. Reduce the heat to medium and cook for a further 5 minutes.

Squash & Spinach Curry

This curry is inspired by my favourite in my local pub – it's full of flavour but not too spicy. Real Indian curries tend to use lots of spices, some of which are quite unusual, so I've tried to make it as simple as possible. If you don't already have cumin, cloves or cardamoms and don't fancy buying them, simply replace them with an extra teaspoon of curry powder (just make sure it's gluten-free). This is delicious served with boiled basmati rice, poppadums, lime pickle and mango chutney.

3 eggs, separated

100g (3½oz) brown rice flour

60ml (2fl oz) milk

¼ teaspoon salt

sunflower oil, for shallow-frying

800g (1¾lb) sustainably sourced boneless white fish fillets, such as Alaska pollock, cut into large pieces

Whisk the egg whites in a thoroughly clean bowl until they form soft peaks. Using the same whisk, whisk the egg yolks, rice flour, milk and salt in a separate large bowl until well combined. Fold the whites into the yolk mixture to form a thick batter.

Pour oil into a large saucepan to the depth of about 1cm (½ inch) and heat over a medium-high heat to 170–180°C (340–350°F), or until a drop of batter sizzles gently.

Using a fork, dip 2 or 3 pieces of fish in the batter mix until both sides are coated, then very carefully lower them into the hot oil using the fork or a slotted spoon. Fry for 3–5 minutes on each side until the batter is dark golden and the fish is cooked through. Remove with a slotted spoon, drain on kitchen paper and serve while still crispy.

Repeat with the remaining fish and batter, adding more oil if necessary and removing any stray bits of batter with a slotted spoon (or they will start to burn).

VARIATION

You can use water in place of the milk for a dairy-free version of this recipe.

Battered Fish

This tempura-style recipe gives a crunchy coating to fish and doesn't need a deep-fat fryer. Try it served with Simple Tomato Sauce (see page 170) and rice, or with chips and peas in the classic British way.

6 eggs, separated

2 tablespoons pesto

75g (3oz) brown rice flour

150g (5oz) cream cheese

1 tablespoon finely chopped chives

180ml (6fl oz) whipping cream

1 garlic clove, crushed

125g (4oz) smoked salmon, cut into small pieces

2 tablespoons olive oil

Preheat the oven to 180°C/350°F/Gas Mark 4. Line a Swiss roll tin or roasting tin with nonstick baking paper.

Whisk the egg whites in a thoroughly clean bowl until they form soft peaks. In a separate large bowl, whisk together 1 tablespoon of the pesto and the egg yolks until the mixture has doubled in volume. Sift over the flour and add the whisked whites, then gently fold together.

Pour the mixture into the prepared tin and gently smooth the top with a spatula. Bake for 15–20 minutes until just cooked through. Lay a clean tea towel over the roulade and flip it over. Lift off the tin, then gently peel away the paper. Roll up the roulade and tea towel to form a sausage and leave to cool.

Meanwhile, mix together the cream cheese, chives and 2 teaspoons of the cream in a bowl until smooth, then add the garlic. Whip the remaining cream, then add to the garlic mixture and fold together.

When the roulade has cooled, unroll it carefully and spread the cream mixture evenly over the surface, leaving a 2cm (¾ inch) strip uncovered at one short side. Scatter the salmon over the surface, then gently roll up the roulade, starting at the end that has the filling spread to the edge. Place on a serving plate, seam side down, and trim the ends.

Mix together the remaining pesto and oil in a small bowl, then serve the roulade cut into slices and drizzled with the sauce.

Smoked Salmon & Pesto Roulade

As an elegant main course this roulade is hard to beat. It is served cold, so can be made in advance – even the day before if necessary. The pesto sauce is also lovely drizzled across boiled new potatoes.

75g (3oz) gluten-free white bread

75g (3oz) cold unsalted butter, diced

1 small onion, roughly chopped

large handful of dill

grated rind of ½ unwaxed lemon

pinch of salt

500g (1lb) piece of boneless salmon fillet, skin on

Preheat the oven to 160°C/325°F/Gas Mark 3.

Place the bread in a food processor and pulse to form breadcrumbs. Spread out the crumbs in a roasting tin and bake for about 30 minutes, stirring occasionally, until dried out and browned.

Place the crisp crumbs in the food processor with the butter, onion, dill, lemon rind and salt. Blend for a minute or so until the mixture forms a paste, then shape into a ball.

Increase the oven temperature to 200°C/400°F/Gas Mark 6.

Place the breadcrumb mixture on a sheet of clingfilm and, using your hands, flatten into a slab about the same size and shape as the salmon fillet. Cut a piece of foil about 10cm (5 inches) wider and longer than the fish and place it in a roasting tin. Place the salmon in the centre, skin side down, then carefully lift up the crust on the clingfilm and flip it on to the fish. Peel off the clingfilm and pinch the corners of the foil together to form a shallow tray, but don't cover the crust with foil. (This will allow the salmon to steam gently in the buttery juices without drying out, while the crust stays crisp.)

Bake for 25 minutes until the fish is just cooked through and the crust has turned golden brown. Serve immediately.

Salmon with a Dill Crust

This recipe takes a slab of salmon and tops it with a neat crumbed herb crust, a technique I learnt from Gordon Ramsay's lovely book, *A Chef for All Seasons*. It looks impressive but is actually very simple – the most time-consuming part of the process is drying out the breadcrumbs, for which you'll need to allow half an hour. Serve with steamed slices of courgette.

SERVES 4

600g (1¼lb) floury potatoes, such as Desiree, scrubbed (or peeled, if preferred) and cubed

60ml (2fl oz) olive oil

50g (2oz) unsalted butter

2 carrots, peeled and finely grated

1 leek, trimmed and finely sliced

2 eggs

350g (11½oz) sustainably sourced white fish fillet, such as cod or Alaska pollock, cut into 3 pieces

500ml (17fl oz) milk

40g (1½oz) cornflour

50g (2oz) Cheddar cheese, grated

sea salt

Preheat the oven to 180°C/350°F/Gas Mark 4.

Cook the potatoes in a large saucepan of boiling water for about 10–15 minutes or until tender, then drain. Roughly mash with the olive oil and set aside.

Meanwhile, melt half the butter in a small saucepan, add the carrots and leek and fry gently for about 8 minutes until soft, then transfer to a 22cm (9 inch) square baking dish.

Rinse out the pan, then add the eggs, cover with cold water and bring to the boil. Cook for about 6–7 minutes until hard-boiled, then cool under cold running water.

While the eggs are cooking, place the fish pieces in another pan, pour in the milk and poach the fish gently for about 5 minutes until cooked through. Drain the fish, reserving the cooking liquid, then remove any skin and bones and flake the flesh into the baking dish.

Using the poaching pan, make the sauce. Melt the remaining butter, then stir in the cornflour and whisk until it forms a lump-free paste. Gradually pour in the reserved milk and the cheese, whisking continuously. Increase the heat and continue to whisk until the sauce thickens. Pour it over the fish.

Shell the eggs and roughly chop, then add to the baking dish and stir until well combined. Spread the mashed potato over the top and sprinkle with sea salt. Bake for 30 minutes until browned and heated through.

Fish Pie

This fish pie elevates a simple piece of white fish into a feast. You'll need three pans, but don't let it put you off because it is well worth the extra washing up. I particularly like this pie with a good helping of peas.

70g (2½oz) gluten-free cornflakes

35g (1oz) rice flour

2 teaspoons gluten-free vegetable stock powder

1 egg

2 tablespoons milk

300g (10oz) dense sustainably sourced skinless white fish fillet, such as Alaska pollock, cut into 8 x 3cm (3 x 1½ inch) fingers

1 tablespoon sunflower oil

Preheat the oven to 160°C/325°F/Gas Mark 3.

Place the cornflakes, rice flour and vegetable stock powder in a food processor and blitz to a fine powder, then tip on to a plate. Beat together the egg and milk and pour into a shallow dish.

Dip each finger of fish first in the egg mixture, then in the crumbs, turning them over until fully coated. Place on a baking sheet and drizzle with the oil. Using tongs, move the fish fingers about, turning them over until both sides are lightly coated in the oil.

Bake for 15 minutes until the coating is crispy and the fish is cooked through.

Fish Fingers

This is a very simple way to create a golden crunchy crumb on fish using cornflakes and a few store-cupboard staples. Get your fishmonger to prepare the fish for you – to make finger shapes, you'll need a piece of fish about 1cm (½ inch) thick, with the skin removed.

100g (3½oz) gluten-free white bread

50g (2oz) unsalted butter, softened

2 teaspoons garlic purée

2 teaspoons chopped parsley

4 boneless, skinless chicken breasts, about 200g (7oz) each

1 egg

Preheat the oven to 160°C/325°F/Gas Mark 3.

Place the bread in a food processor and pulse to form breadcrumbs. Spread out the crumbs in a roasting tin and bake for about 30 minutes, stirring occasionally, until dried out and browned.

Meanwhile, make the filling. Place the butter, garlic purée and parsley in a small bowl and stir together. Shape the mixture into marble-sized lumps, then place the bowl in the freezer.

Lay 1 chicken breast on a clean work surface. Using a small, sharp knife, make a horizontal cut about 2cm (1 inch) long in the underside of the breast – aim for the thickest part of the breast, about a third of the way down. Carefully (so you don't puncture any further holes or indeed your own hand) wiggle the knife about to create a pocket as large as possible – try not to enlarge the initial cut while you do this. Alternatively, create the pocket using your finger. Repeat with the remaining chicken breasts.

Insert 3 or 4 lumps of the butter into each pocket. Skewer the cuts shut with cocktail sticks – if you accidentally make holes elsewhere, skewer those shut as well. Cover and chill the chicken breasts for 15–30 minutes.

Beat the egg on a large plate. Tip the breadcrumbs on to another plate. Dip each chicken breast into the egg, then the crumbs, turning to coat both sides.

Transfer the coated breasts to a baking sheet and bake for 30 minutes until the chicken is golden and cooked through. Remove the cocktail sticks before serving.

Chicken Kiev

Chicken Kiev has been a favourite for hundreds of years, thanks to its crispy coating and oozing buttery garlic centre. Invented by a Russian chef, it was once fancily named Côtelettes de Volaille, and even formed part of Queen Victoria's Christmas Day menu in 1899.

2 tablespoons olive oil

4 chicken thighs, skin on

1 garlic clove, finely chopped

1 tablespoon sweet paprika

pinch of saffron threads

125g (4oz) runner beans, trimmed and sliced into 3cm (1½ inch) lengths

2 tomatoes, finely chopped

400g (13oz) can cannellini beans, rinsed and drained

6 canned artichoke hearts, finely chopped

2 rosemary sprigs, finely chopped, plus extra sprigs to garnish

1 teaspoon salt

625ml (1 pint) water

250g (8oz) Bomba or Calasparra rice

Heat the oil in a 30cm (12 inch) paella pan or frying pan over a medium-high heat. Add the chicken thighs and cook for 2 minutes on each side until browned.

Add the garlic, sweet paprika, saffron, runner beans and tomatoes, reduce the heat to medium and cook gently for 2 minutes. Stir in the cannellini beans, artichokes, rosemary and salt, then gradually pour in the measurement water. Add the rice and stir, increasing the heat a little until the liquid starts to bubble.

Simmer without stirring for about 10 minutes, then flip the chicken pieces over and cook for a further 10 minutes or until the chicken is cooked through and the rice has absorbed most of the liquid – the rice will gradually form a crust at the bottom (the socarrat, considered a particular delicacy).

Remove the pan from the heat and leave to stand for 5 minutes. Garnish the chicken with extra sprigs of rosemary, then carry the pan to the table to serve.

Chicken Paella

Tradition dictates that paella should be made in an enormously wide pan on an open fire, by a man. I've obviously broken all the rules by making mine in a 30cm (12 inch) frying pan in my kitchen, but feel free to stick to the traditions as you see fit. The rice is important: paella rices like Bomba and Calasparra swell while keeping their grains distinct; risotto rices become creamy. If you can't find paella rice, use a generic short-grain rice instead.

SERVES 4

100g (3½oz) gluten-free white bread

2 teaspoons paprika

1 tablespoon gluten-free vegetable stock powder

1 egg

4 boneless, skinless chicken breasts, about 150g (5oz) each, cut into 2cm (¾ inch) cubes

2 teaspoons sunflower oil

VARIATION

You can make these nuggets dairy-free, too: use stock powder and bread that are dairy-free as well as gluten-free, and use soya milk if you want to pre-soak the chicken breasts.

Preheat the oven to 160°C/325°F/Gas Mark 3.

Place the bread in a food processor and pulse to form breadcrumbs. Spread out the crumbs in a roasting tin and bake for about 30 minutes, stirring occasionally, until dried out and browned.

Transfer the dried breadcrumbs to a food processor, add the paprika and vegetable stock powder and pulse a few times until the mixture resembles sand. Pour it into a large plastic bag and set aside.

Beat the egg in a medium-sized bowl. Add the chicken to the bowl in batches, stirring to ensure each piece is evenly coated. Lift the pieces out with a slotted spoon and drop them into the bag with the crumb mixture. Hold the bag firmly shut and then shake it to coat the chicken. Lift out each piece using tongs. Repeat until all the chicken has been coated. (The nuggets can either be frozen or cooked at this stage.)

Increase the oven temperature to 180°C/350°F/Gas Mark 4. Drizzle the oil on to a baking sheet. Place the nuggets on the sheet, then stir them around slightly until lightly coated in the oil. Bake for about 15 minutes (or 20–25 minutes from frozen) until the coating is golden and the chicken is cooked through.

Chicken Nuggets

These chicken nuggets are surprisingly quick and easy to make and require no deep-frying. The uncooked nuggets freeze well, too. You can serve them with chips or potato wedges, but they also make a great meal served with gluten-free spaghetti and Simple Tomato Sauce (see page 170). If you want extra-juicy nuggets, soak the chicken breasts in milk overnight before you chop them up.

SERVES 4

1½ tablespoons olive oil

1 onion, finely chopped

4 garlic cloves, finely chopped

1 red chilli, deseeded and cut into very thin strips

1 teaspoon gluten-free ground cinnamon

400ml (14fl oz) can coconut milk

1 tablespoon tomato purée

juice of 1 lime

500g (1lb) boneless, skinless chicken breasts, cut into thin strips

1 teaspoon soft dark brown sugar

6 cherry tomatoes, halved

100g (3½oz) fine green beans, trimmed

75g (3oz) fresh coriander, chopped

salt

Heat the oil in a large pan over a medium heat, add the onion, garlic, chilli and cinnamon and fry gently for about 5 minutes until the onion has softened.

Stir in half the coconut milk, the tomato purée and lime juice, then add the chicken, sugar and cherry tomatoes. Bring to the boil, then reduce the heat and simmer gently, uncovered, for about 15 minutes or until the chicken is cooked through. Season to taste with salt.

Add the green beans to the pan, then gradually stir in the remaining coconut milk until the sauce is the consistency of cream. Cook for a further 5 minutes, then remove the pan from the heat and stir in the chopped coriander.

VARIATION
This curry is also delicious made with fillets of white fish instead of chicken.

Coconut & Lime Chicken Curry

This chicken curry is inspired by flavours commonly used in dishes from Thailand and the west coast of India: garlic, tomato, lime and coconut, all mixed up with plenty of fresh coriander. Serve it with boiled white rice or jasmine rice.

1 quantity gluten-free Plain Shortcrust Pastry (see page 166)

cornflour, for dusting

4 teaspoons tomato purée

2 teaspoons olive oil

6 smoked streaky bacon rashers, cut into small pieces

125g (4oz) broccoli, roughly chopped

3 eggs

170ml (6fl oz) single cream

85ml (3fl oz) milk

salt and pepper

Preheat the oven to 180°C/350°F/Gas Mark 4.

Roll out the pastry to about 4mm (¼ inch) thick on a work surface well dusted with cornflour. Line a 20cm (8 inch) tart tin with the pastry and trim any excess using a sharp knife. Spread the tomato purée over the base of the pastry case, then sprinkle with a little salt.

Heat the oil in a nonstick frying pan, add the bacon and fry for about 5 minutes until any water has evaporated and it is golden brown and slightly crunchy.

Meanwhile, boil or steam the broccoli until very tender. Drain, if necessary, and leave to cool slightly, then finely chop.

Scatter the cooked bacon and broccoli over the pastry case.

Beat the eggs in a jug, then whisk in the cream, milk and a little salt and pepper. Pour into the pastry case and bake for 30 minutes until browned and the filling is completely set.

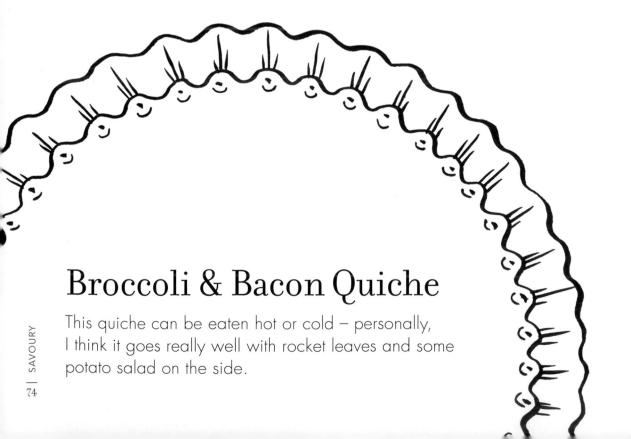

Broccoli & Bacon Quiche

This quiche can be eaten hot or cold – personally, I think it goes really well with rocket leaves and some potato salad on the side.

150g (5oz) gluten-free white
bread

2 teaspoons paprika

1 tablespoon gluten-free
vegetable stock powder

1 egg

600g (1¼lb) pork loin steaks,
trimmed

2 tablespoons sunflower oil

Preheat the oven to 160°C/325°F/Gas Mark 3.

Place the bread in a food processor and pulse to form
breadcrumbs. Spread out the crumbs in a roasting tin
and bake for about 20 minutes, stirring occasionally,
until dried out.

Place the crisp crumbs in the food processor with the
paprika and vegetable stock powder. Pulse a few times to
form a sand-like mixture. Tip on to a large plate. Beat the
egg on another large plate.

One at a time, place each pork steak between 2 sheets
of clingfilm or baking paper, then bang vigorously with
a rolling pin until no more than 1cm (½ inch) thick.

Using a fork, dip the pork pieces in the egg, then in the
breadcrumbs, turning until well coated on both sides.

Heat the sunflower oil in a nonstick frying pan over a
medium heat and fry the escalopes for 3–4 minutes on
each side or until cooked through, crispy and golden brown.
Drain on kitchen paper and serve hot or cold.

VARIATION
To make a dairy-free version of this recipe,
choose bread and stock powder that are dairy-free
as well as gluten-free.

Breaded Pork Escalopes

Whether you call them escalopes or schnitzel, these thin pieces
of breaded pork make excellent sandwich fillings, or can simply
be served with a wedge of lemon and a sprinkling of parsley.

1.5kg (3lb) boned ham joint

1 pineapple

40g (1½oz) soft dark brown sugar

2 teaspoons gluten-free mustard

1 teaspoon cornflour

2 tablespoons orange juice

Place the ham in a large stockpot or saucepan and cover with cold water. Leave to soak overnight, then discard the water.

Cover the ham with fresh water and bring to the boil, then reduce the heat and simmer for 45 minutes until the ham is cooked through, skimming the surface with a metal spoon. Drain the ham and leave to cool slightly.

Meanwhile, cut away the pineapple skin and leaves and remove the core – if you want classic pineapple rings, use a pineapple corer or small serrated knife. Finely dice 50g (2oz) of the pineapple and set aside. Slice the remainder into pieces about 1cm (½ inch) thick, then arrange in a roasting tin.

Place the diced pineapple in a small saucepan, add the brown sugar, mustard and cornflour and heat gently until the mixture thickens. Set aside.

Preheat the oven to 180°C/350°F/Gas Mark 4. Place the cooled ham on a chopping board and remove any string. Using a very sharp knife, remove the skin and most of the fat until a 2–3mm (⅛ inch) layer of fat remains. Score this into a diamond pattern with the tip of the knife. You may want to retie some cook's string around the ham. Place the ham on the sliced pineapple in the roasting tin.

Spread a thick layer of the diced pineapple mixture over the top of the ham, then roast for 45–60 minutes until the top is darkened and sticky. Remove from the oven and place on a carving board.

Add the orange juice to the juices in the roasting tin and stir well. Slice the ham and serve with the roast pineapple and a drizzle of orange sauce.

Roast Pineapple & Mustard Ham

Pineapple, brown sugar and mustard create a spicy, chewy topping for a roast joint of ham and also form the basis of a tangy orange sauce to serve alongside. It's wonderful for a special occasion, but also easy enough to make for a regular weekend.

2 carrots, peeled and roughly chopped

2 celery sticks, roughly chopped

1 onion, quartered

2 tablespoons olive oil

800g (1¾lb) lean minced beef

2 x 400g (13oz) cans chopped tomatoes

60ml (2fl oz) gluten-free tomato ketchup

60ml (2fl oz) red wine

¼ teaspoon salt

3 courgettes, about 400g (13oz) total weight

25g (1oz) unsalted butter

20g (³⁄₁₀oz) cornflour

375ml (13fl oz) milk

50g (2oz) Cheddar cheese, grated

Place the carrots, celery and onion in a food processor and blitz until finely minced. Alternatively, chop the vegetables very finely.

Heat half the oil in a saucepan, add the beef and fry for about 10 minutes, breaking it up with a wooden spoon, until browned and cooked through. Drain off any liquid and transfer the beef to a bowl. Set aside.

Heat the remaining oil in the pan, add the minced vegetables and fry gently for about 5 minutes until softened. Add the cooked beef, tomatoes, ketchup, wine and salt and simmer for 1 hour.

Meanwhile, slice the courgettes lengthways into very thin ribbons (use a mandolin, if you have one), then steam until just tender and drain.

When you are ready to assemble the lasagne, preheat the oven to 160°C/325°F/Gas Mark 3. Melt the butter in a saucepan, then stir in the cornflour and whisk until lump-free. Gradually add the milk, stirring until smooth. Bring to the boil, whisking continuously until the sauce is thickened.

Spread half the meat mixture in a 30 x 23cm (12 x 9 inch) lasagne dish and cover with half the courgette strips. Repeat with the remaining meat and courgettes. Pour over the white sauce and sprinkle the cheese on top. Bake for 50 minutes until the cheese is browned.

Low-carb Lasagne

Few dishes are as appealing as home-cooked lasagne, straight from the oven. Even better, thinly sliced courgette takes the place of pasta for this version, making it very low in carbohydrates.

2 teaspoons cornflour

425g (15oz) can pineapple chunks
in juice

60ml (2fl oz) gluten-free tomato
ketchup

1 tablespoon cider vinegar

1 teaspoon salt

2 balls stem ginger from a jar of
stem ginger in syrup, finely diced

2 tablespoons olive oil

400g (13oz) pork, trimmed and
cut into pencil-thick strips

1 onion, sliced

8 spring onions, cut diagonally
into 2cm (¾ inch) lengths

1 yellow pepper, cored, deseeded
and cut into thin batons

1 carrot, peeled and cut into
batons

4 garlic cloves, finely chopped

100g (3½oz) mangetout, trimmed

Place the cornflour in a jug and gradually stir in all the juice
from the can of pineapple. Add the ketchup, vinegar, salt and
1 tablespoon syrup from the stem ginger jar and mix well.

Heat the oil in a wok or large frying pan until it is hot. Add the
pork, onion, spring onions, yellow pepper, carrot, garlic and
stem ginger and stir-fry for 2 minutes or until the pork is just
cooked through. Stir in the cornflour mixture and cook for
a further few minutes.

Stir in the pineapple chunks and mangetout and continue
to stir-fry for 2 minutes or until heated through, then
serve immediately.

Sweet & Sour Pork

Prepared Chinese sauces almost always contain soy sauce, which
also contains wheat flour. This quick and easy sweet and sour pork
is full of colourful, crunchy vegetables and is made without soy
sauce, but you'd never notice the difference. Serve with rice.

8 fat leeks

2 teaspoons olive oil

400g (13oz) pancetta or chopped bacon

250g (8oz) ricotta cheese

2 x 400g (13oz) cans chopped tomatoes

2 x 250g (8oz) balls buffalo mozzarella cheese, torn into chunks

2 teaspoons dried oregano

sea salt

Preheat the oven to 180°C/350°F/Gas Mark 4.

Trim the leeks and remove the outer layer. Rinse out as much grit as you can without cutting into the leeks. Fit the leeks into a stockpot or large pan, cover with boiling water and cook for about 10 minutes until soft. Drain and rinse under cold running water until cool enough to handle, then push out the centres to form 8 leek tubes. Take the 4 fattest removed centres and push out the centres again to form another 4 leek tubes. Set the 12 tubes to one side and put the cooked leek centres in a food processor.

Heat the oil in a frying pan, add the pancetta or bacon and cook for 4–5 minutes until well cooked, but not crispy. Add to the food processor with the ricotta. Pulse a few times until fully chopped but retaining some texture – you don't want a purée.

Scoop the mixture into a plastic food bag and cut off one of the corners, then pipe into the leek tubes.

Place the filled leeks in a large ovenproof dish and top with the tomatoes. Half-fill 1 empty tomato can with water and add to the dish. Scatter over the mozzarella, followed by the dried oregano and a sprinkling of salt.

Bake for 35–40 minutes until heated through and the mozzarella is golden brown. Serve.

Leek & Pancetta Cannelloni

If you push the centres out of large leeks you end up with thin tubes that are a nutritious substitute for cannelloni pasta. They have the bonus of being very low in carbohydrates. The leek tubes can be used for a variety of fillings, but for this recipe I've mixed the remainder of the leek with pancetta and ricotta to make an Italian-inspired bake.

SERVES 4

sunflower oil, for greasing

100g (3½oz) gluten-free bread, crusts removed

60ml (2fl oz) milk

400g (13oz) lean minced beef

1 teaspoon salt

½ teaspoon gluten-free ground allspice

½ teaspoon ground black pepper

Preheat the oven to 180°C/350°F/Gas Mark 4. Generously grease a baking sheet with sunflower oil.

Roughly crumble the bread into a large bowl and add the milk. Stir together until smooth and well mixed. Add the beef, salt, allspice and pepper and, using your hands, mix together well.

Roll about 1 tablespoon of the meat mixture into a ball and place on the prepared baking sheet. Repeat with the remaining mixture to make about 35 meatballs. Roll the meatballs around on the sheet to coat lightly in the oil.

Bake for 25–30 minutes until crisp on the outside and soft but cooked through inside. Serve hot.

Swedish Meatballs

Swedish meatballs are characterized by their softness, the secret of which is breadcrumbs soaked in milk. Serve Swedish-style, with gravy made by stirring 60ml (2fl oz) single cream into 250ml (8fl oz) thickened beef gravy (add salt to taste), boiled new potatoes and a dollop of lingonberry or cranberry sauce alongside. Alternatively, try them on gluten-free spaghetti with Simple Tomato Sauce (see page 170).

1 tablespoon olive oil

1 small onion, finely chopped

500g (1lb) minced beef

100g (3½oz) mushrooms, diced

1 red pepper, cored, deseeded
and diced

1 tablespoon smoked paprika

2 teaspoons chopped oregano

1 teaspoon gluten-free instant
coffee

1 small green chilli, deseeded
and finely chopped (optional)

400g (13oz) can kidney beans,
rinsed and drained

2 x 400g (13oz) cans chopped
tomatoes

60ml (2fl oz) water

Heat the oil in a large saucepan, add the onion and fry gently for 5 minutes until softened. Add the beef and cook for about 10 minutes, breaking it up with a spoon, until browned and almost cooked through.

Add the mushrooms and red pepper, then stir in the smoked paprika, oregano, coffee and green chilli, if using. Add the kidney beans, tomatoes and measurement water (rinse out the empty tomato cans with the water before adding), then stir well and bring to the boil.

Reduce the heat to medium-low, cover with a lid and simmer for 2 hours, stirring occasionally, to let the flavours develop.

Chilli

Chilli is real one-pot food, great for those times when you want to keep preparation to a minimum. This version uses smoked paprika, oregano and coffee to make a rich sauce that isn't too hot, but if you're not fond of spicy food, just omit the chilli. Serve with corn tacos or homemade Corn Tortillas (see page 179).

MAKES 6

1 onion, quartered

400g (13oz) lean minced beef

¼ teaspoon salt

¼ teaspoon ground black pepper

olive oil, for frying (optional)

Place the onion in a food processor and blitz until minced, then tip into a bowl with the beef and mix together. Add the salt and pepper, then mix together using your hands.

Divide the mixture into 6 equal-sized portions and shape into patties about 1cm (½ inch) thick.

You can now either shallow-fry the burgers in a little olive oil or barbecue them until cooked through. About 2–3 minutes on each side is usually sufficient. To check if the burgers are cooked through, cut one open – no pink should remain.

Beefburgers

Shop-bought beefburgers often have wheat flour as an added ingredient, making them unsuitable for people avoiding gluten. Luckily, burgers are surprisingly quick and easy to make at home. Use good-quality beef and there's no need for fillers.

SWEET

SERVES 4–6

100g (3½oz) unsalted butter, melted, plus extra for greasing

100g (3½oz) Gluten-free Plain White Flour Blend (see page 164)

100g (3½oz) granulated sugar

50g (2oz) desiccated coconut

1 teaspoon gluten-free baking powder

pinch of salt

1 egg, lightly beaten

2 cooking apples, about 400g (13oz) total weight, peeled, cored and sliced

2 teaspoons demerara sugar

1 teaspoon gluten-free ground cinnamon

Preheat the oven to 160°C/325°F/Gas Mark 3. Grease a 22cm (9 inch) springform cake tin with butter.

Place the flour blend, sugar, coconut, baking powder and salt in a bowl. Pour the melted butter into the dry ingredients and stir well. Add the egg and mix until well combined.

Spread the mixture evenly in the prepared cake tin. Arrange the apples on top and sprinkle with the demerara sugar and cinnamon. Bake for 50 minutes until the apples are golden and the base is shrinking from the sides of the tin. (The tart will be quite delicate when hot, but becomes more robust as it cools.) Serve warm or cold.

VARIATION

Use 100g (3½oz) dairy-free margarine instead of butter for a dairy-free version of this recipe.

Apple & Coconut Tart

My mother's friend Rie introduced me to this quick and easy tart. I immediately fell in love with its sharp apple topping and the subtly coconut-flavoured base that is crunchy on the outside and chewy within. Serve warm or cold with crème fraîche.

125g (4oz) gluten-free sweet
plain hard biscuits

75g (3oz) unsalted butter

½ teaspoon gluten-free
ground ginger

200g (7oz) cream cheese

125ml (4fl oz) single cream

75g (3oz) icing sugar, sifted

pinch of salt

2 eggs, separated

Rhubarb sauce

350g (11½oz) rhubarb, trimmed
and cut into 1cm (½ inch) pieces

50g (2oz) granulated sugar, plus
extra if needed

60ml (2fl oz) water

2 balls from a jar of stem ginger
in syrup, about 25g (1oz), finely
diced

Place the biscuits in a sealed plastic food bag and bash with
a rolling pin to form crumbs. Alternatively, blitz them in a
food processor. Melt 50g (2oz) of the butter in a small saucepan,
then stir in the biscuit crumbs and ground ginger until well
combined. Tip the crumbs into a deep 20cm (8 inch) loose-
bottomed tart tin or springform tin and smooth the mixture
level using the back of a metal tablespoon.

Preheat the oven to 200°C/400°F/Gas Mark 6. To make the
filling, melt the remaining butter and pour into a large bowl.
Add the cream cheese and stir until smooth. Gradually add the
cream, followed by the icing sugar and salt.

Stir the egg yolks into the cream cheese mixture. Whisk the
egg whites in a thoroughly clean bowl until they form firm
peaks, then fold into the cheese mixture.

Pour the mixture on to the biscuit base and bake for 10 minutes,
then reduce the oven temperature to 160°C/325°F/Gas Mark 3
and cook for a further 35 minutes until a skewer inserted into
the centre comes out clean and the cheesecake is risen and
browned. (The filling will sink as it cools, but this is normal.)

To make the sauce, place all the ingredients in a saucepan and
simmer gently for about 15 minutes until the rhubarb is tender
and starting to disintegrate, but retains some texture. Add a
little more sugar to the sauce, if liked. Serve the sauce hot or
cold with the warm or chilled cheesecake. To serve the cake
chilled, transfer it to a large plate. If serving the cake warm,
leave it in the tart tin, as it's tricky to transfer.

Baked Cheesecake
with Rhubarb & Ginger

Based on a traditional American recipe, this cheesecake has
a dark, undulating crust and a slightly wobbly centre. Its creamy
flavour and soufflé-like texture marry well with the spiced rhubarb
sauce – I love the bright pink of new-season rhubarb, in particular.

150g (5oz) unsalted butter, plus extra for greasing

150g (5oz) granulated sugar

125ml (4fl oz) water

1 teaspoon vanilla extract

200g (7oz) Gluten-free Plain White Flour Blend (see page 164)

70g (2½oz) ground almonds

2 teaspoons gluten-free baking powder

pinch of salt

4 eggs, lightly beaten

icing sugar, for dusting

Filling

125ml (4fl oz) whipping cream

150g (5oz) strawberries, hulled

2 tablespoons strawberry jam

Preheat the oven to 150°C/300°F/Gas Mark 2. Lightly grease 2 x 20cm (8 inch) sandwich tins with butter.

Place the butter, sugar, measurement water and vanilla extract in a saucepan and cook over a medium-high heat until the butter melts. Add the flour blend and then whisk continuously – the mixture will thicken and may stick to the base of the pan, so keep whisking to prevent it burning (don't worry about small lumps at this stage). When a thick paste forms, remove the pan from the heat and keep whisking for a further 20 seconds, then set aside.

In a large bowl, stir together the ground almonds, baking powder and salt. Pour in the paste and add the eggs. Whisk together for 1 minute (use a hand-held electric whisk if you have one), then divide the mixture evenly between the cake tins. Bake for 25 minutes until risen, golden and a skewer inserted into the centre comes out clean. Leave to cool in the tins.

Whip the cream until soft peaks form. Reserve 2 tablespoons of the cream and 8 strawberries for decoration. Slice the remaining strawberries and stir into the jam.

Spread the cream across the top of one cake, followed by the strawberry mixture. Sandwich together with the remaining cake and dust with icing sugar. Decorate with the reserved cream and strawberries.

Strawberry Sponge Cake

This cake uses a slightly unusual method, but the result is a light and extremely soft vanilla sponge that is perfectly matched by the filling of cream, jam and fresh strawberries.

75g (3oz) unsalted butter, softened, plus extra for greasing

100g (3½oz) granulated sugar

2 eggs, lightly beaten

75g (3oz) brown rice flour

70g (2½oz) ground almonds

2 teaspoons gluten-free baking powder

grated rind of 2 unwaxed lemons

1 tablespoon milk

Topping

juice of 1 lemon

50g (2oz) granulated sugar

Preheat the oven to 170°C/340°F/Gas Mark 3½. Lightly grease a 22cm (9 inch) loaf tin with butter.

Place the butter and sugar in a bowl and beat together for about 1 minute with a hand-held electric whisk until light and fluffy. Add the eggs, rice flour, ground almonds and baking powder and beat together for a few seconds until combined. Add the lemon rind and milk, then beat again.

Spoon the mixture into the prepared tin and shake slightly to make sure the mixture is evenly distributed. Bake for 40 minutes until a skewer inserted into the centre comes out clean.

Meanwhile, mix together the lemon juice and sugar in a cup (the sugar won't dissolve, but that is normal).

Leaving the cake in the tin, lightly prick the top all over with a fork, then evenly pour over the lemon juice mixture while the cake is still hot. Leave to cool in the tin before serving.

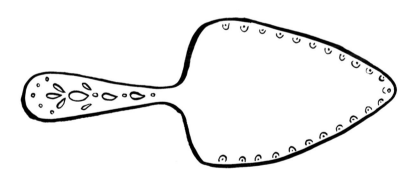

Lemon Drizzle Cake

The combination of crunchy sugar topping and lemon-soaked sponge makes this loaf cake a perennial teatime favourite; it is also a fine dessert if you serve each slice with a scoop of raspberry sorbet. It'll keep for a couple of days in an airtight container.

75g (3oz) unsalted butter, diced, plus extra for greasing

380g (12oz) gooseberries, trimmed

70g (2½oz) granulated sugar

60ml (2fl oz) elderflower cordial

125ml (4fl oz) natural yogurt

150g (5oz) ground almonds

70g (2½oz) cornmeal

2 eggs, lightly beaten

1 teaspoon bicarbonate of soda

1 teaspoon gluten-free baking powder

pinch of salt

Icing

50g (2oz) icing sugar, sifted

2 teaspoons elderflower cordial

1 teaspoon lemon juice

Preheat the oven to 180°C/350°F/Gas Mark 4. Lightly grease a 22cm (9 inch) springform cake tin with butter.

Place the gooseberries, sugar and cordial in a saucepan over a medium heat and gently cook until the sugar has dissolved and the fruit is tender. Leave to cool for about 10 minutes, then purée with a hand-held blender or in a food processor or blender. Stir in the butter and leave to melt.

Pour the mixture into a large bowl, add the yogurt, ground almonds, cornmeal, eggs, bicarbonate of soda, baking powder and salt and stir until combined. Quickly spoon the mixture into the prepared tin and bake for 40 minutes until well browned and firm to the touch. Leave to cool completely in the tin.

To make the icing, mix together the icing sugar, cordial and lemon juice in a bowl. Run a knife round the edges of the tin and transfer the cake to a serving plate. Drizzle over the icing and leave to set for at least 1 hour before serving.

Gooseberry & Elderflower Cake

With its combination of juicy gooseberries and fragrant elderflower, this moist and simple cake captures the essence of a warm day. But it need not be summer when you make it because it works just as well with frozen berries and cordial from the store cupboard. It'll keep for a couple of days in an airtight container.

2 tablespoons sunflower oil,
plus extra for greasing

140g (5oz) walnut pieces, plus
3 walnut halves for decorating

75g (3oz) brown rice flour

55g (2oz) soft dark brown sugar

125ml (4fl oz) milk

2 eggs, lightly beaten

1 teaspoon vanilla extract

2 teaspoons instant coffee

3 teaspoons boiling water

2 teaspoons gluten-free baking
powder

Buttercream

1 teaspoon instant coffee

2 teaspoons boiling water

75g (3oz) icing sugar, sifted

50g (2oz) unsalted butter,
softened

Icing

½ teaspoon instant coffee

2 teaspoons boiling water

50g (2oz) icing sugar, sifted

Preheat the oven to 170°C/340°F/Gas Mark 3½. Lightly oil a 22cm (9 inch) loaf tin with sunflower oil.

Place 100g (3½oz) of the walnut pieces and the rice flour in a food processor and process until the mixture is the texture of coffee grinds. Add the brown sugar, milk, oil, eggs and vanilla extract. Stir together the instant coffee and measurement boiling water in a small cup until the coffee dissolves. Pour into the food processor and blend for 1 minute until the mixture is thick and creamy. Leave to stand for 15 minutes.

Add the baking powder to the cake mixture and blend for a couple of seconds. Fold in the remaining walnut pieces, then pour into the prepared loaf tin, smoothing the top with a spatula. Bake for 30 minutes until an inserted skewer comes out clean. Leave to cool in the tin.

To make the buttercream filling, mix together the coffee and measurement boiling water in a large bowl, then stir in the icing sugar. Add the butter and beat until well combined.

Cut the cooled cake in half horizontally using a sharp knife (I find a bread knife works best). Evenly spread the base with the buttercream, then sandwich together with the top.

To make the icing, mix together the coffee and measurement boiling water in a bowl until completely dissolved (or you'll get dark flecks in your icing). Stir in the icing sugar to form a thick mixture. Spread across the top of the cake using a palette knife, then decorate with the walnut halves. Chill for 1 hour before serving.

Coffee & Walnut Cake

Coffee and walnut is a wonderful flavour combination. I've used ground walnuts in place of much of the flour, which makes this cake a more nutritious treat. The natural oiliness of the walnuts reduces the need for added fats.

SERVES 4

4 cooking apples, about 800g (1¾ lb) total weight, peeled, cored and cut into small chunks

2 teaspoons water

4 teaspoons granulated sugar, plus extra if needed

100g (3½oz) unsalted butter

110g (3½oz) soft light brown sugar

200g (7oz) gluten-free cornflakes

Place the apples, measurement water and granulated sugar in a saucepan and cook over a low heat for about 15–20 minutes until the apples have softened and are still a little sour but not eye-wateringly so — add more sugar to taste if necessary. Leave to cool.

Meanwhile, melt the butter in a large frying pan over a low heat, add the brown sugar and stir until the sugar dissolves. Increase the heat slightly and add the cornflakes. Using a spoon, crush them gently and stir for a few minutes until well coated in the butter mixture. Leave to cool, stirring occasionally to prevent the flakes clumping together.

To serve, alternate layers of apple and cornflakes evenly among 4 dessert glasses. Serve immediately.

Crunchy Cornflake Apple Pudding

Buttery, toffee-flavoured crunchy cornflakes are layered sundae-style with soft and slightly tart stewed apple in this tasty dessert. It's one of my mother's inventions and is a regular feature of autumn at home, thanks to the tree in the garden. While the apple and buttered cornflakes can be made in advance, the dessert needs to be assembled just before it is served or you'll end up with a soggy mess. Delicious with crème fraîche or whipped cream.

50g (2oz) tapioca flour

125ml (4fl oz) milk

60ml (2fl oz) hand-hot water

1 teaspoon fast-action dried yeast

2 teaspoons granulated sugar

75g (3oz) Gluten-free Plain
White Flour Blend (see page 164),
plus extra for dusting

50g (2oz) ground almonds

2 teaspoons sunflower oil

pinch of salt

25g (1oz) unsalted butter, softened

40g (1½oz) soft light brown sugar

1 teaspoon gluten-free ground
cinnamon

Place the tapioca flour and milk in a saucepan and heat gently, stirring, until it comes together as a very sticky white lump. Remove the pan from the heat.

Stir together the warm measurement water, yeast and granulated sugar in a cup and leave to stand for a few minutes until the mixture starts to froth.

Place the flour blend, ground almonds, oil and salt in a large bowl. Pour in the yeasty liquid, then add the tapioca mixture to the bowl and, using a spoon, turn the lump over until it is well coated in flour. Knead together for at least 1 minute until well combined and the dough is slightly oily. Turn the dough out on to a work surface lightly dusted with flour blend and spread out to a rough rectangle, about 24 x 18cm (9½ x 7 inches).

Mix together the butter, brown sugar and cinnamon in a small bowl, then spread the mixture evenly across the dough. Starting at one of the narrow ends, roll up the dough and cut into 6 slices.

Place the rounds, spiral side up, in a small roasting tin, about 18 x 13cm (7 x 5 inches). Loosely cover the dish with clingfilm and leave to rise in a warm place for at least 1½ hours until the slices have puffed up and filled the tin.

Preheat the oven to 160°C/325°F/Gas Mark 3. Bake the buns for 40 minutes until golden brown. Serve warm.

Cinnamon Spiral Buns

The smell of sweet cinnamon buns baking is the epitome of cosiness – and probably why they are so popular across Scandinavia. If you want to eat these for breakfast, I recommend making them the night before and baking them for 30 minutes; the final 10 minutes of baking can then be carried out in the morning in order to enjoy them fresh from the oven.

butter, for greasing

2 teaspoons granulated sugar

400g (13oz) fresh cherries, rinsed and pitted

40g (1½oz) cornflour

250ml (8fl oz) single cream, plus extra to serve

50g (2oz) ground almonds

80g (3oz) soft light brown sugar

4 eggs

¼ teaspoon almond extract

pinch of salt

Preheat the oven to 170°C/340°F/Gas Mark 3½. Grease a pie dish with butter, then sprinkle with the granulated sugar.

Pat the cherries dry using kitchen paper, then scatter across the pie dish.

Place the cornflour and cream in a bowl and whisk together until smooth. Add the ground almonds, brown sugar, eggs, almond extract and salt. Whisk to combine, then pour into the dish.

Bake for 50–60 minutes until risen, puffy and well browned.

Cherry Clafoutis

Clafoutis is a French dessert featuring fresh cherries baked in a delicious sweet batter – so delicious, in fact, that I am always torn between the joy of eating the cherries raw or cooking them like this. It is definitely one of my top 10 puddings. Serve warm with cream.

1 English Breakfast tea bag

375ml (13fl oz) boiling water

100g (3½oz) gluten-free porridge oats, quinoa flakes or millet flakes

125ml (4fl oz) apple juice

400g (13oz) can prunes in juice

15g (½oz) sunflower seeds

Steep the tea bag in the measurement boiling water for 2 minutes, then pour into a saucepan. Discard the tea bag.

Add the oats, quinoa or millet, the apple juice and the juice from the can of prunes and simmer over a medium heat for about 10 minutes, stirring occasionally, until the mixture thickens.

Stir in the prunes and cook for a further 1 minute, then pour into 2 serving bowls and sprinkle over the sunflower seeds.

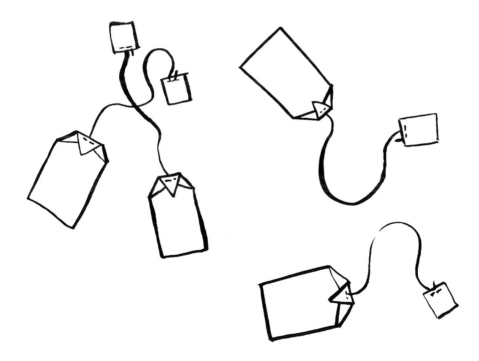

Prune Porridge

Prunes combine with English Breakfast tea to flavour a nutritious porridge of oats, millet or quinoa (my favourite), as you prefer. Just remember to watch out for prune stones!

100g (3½oz) gluten-free
porridge oats

125ml (4fl oz) good-quality
apple juice

125ml (4fl oz) water

125ml (4fl oz) natural yogurt

1 dessert apple, cored and
coarsely grated

15g (½oz) sunflower seeds

15g (½oz) walnut pieces

1 teaspoon linseeds

Place the oats in a large bowl, add the apple juice and
measurement water and leave to soak overnight.

The next morning, stir in the yogurt. Add the apple and
sprinkle over the sunflower seeds, then stir together.

Spoon the muesli into 2 bowls and sprinkle over the
walnut pieces and linseeds.

VARIATION

Redcurrants, raspberries,
blueberries or pomegranate
seeds all taste great sprinkled on
top if you want a bit of variation.
For a dairy-free breakfast, use
soya yogurt instead of the
natural yogurt.

Bircher Muesli

Bircher muesli makes a nutritious start to the day and, apart from
a little forethought (the oats need to soak overnight), is dead easy
to make, and you can dress it up or down as you wish.

60ml (2fl oz) clear honey

2 tablespoons sunflower oil

1 teaspoon gluten-free baking
powder

70g (2½oz) gluten-free plain
puffed rice

100g (3½oz) quinoa flakes

75g (3oz) sunflower seeds

50g (2oz) pumpkin seeds

50g (2oz) walnuts, chopped

50g (2oz) hazelnuts, chopped

Preheat the oven to 160°C/325°F/Gas Mark 3.

Mix together the honey, oil and baking powder in a small
bowl. Place the puffed rice, quinoa flakes, sunflower seeds
and pumpkin seeds in a large roasting tin. Pour over the honey
mixture and stir until all the dry ingredients are well coated.

Roast for 15 minutes, then stir again. Return the tin to the oven
and cook for a further 10 minutes.

Add the nuts to the granola while it is still warm. Give it another
good stir and leave to cool. It will keep for 2 weeks stored in an
airtight container.

Honey-roast Granola

A touch of honey makes this nutritious granola especially tasty.
I love it because it's not only simple to make but also versatile.
I've used walnuts and hazelnuts here, but don't feel limited by this:
they can easily be substituted with the same weight of other nuts
or dried fruit, depending on your preferences and store-cupboard
contents (Brazil nuts and chopped dried apricots are another great
pairing). Try the granola drenched with apple or orange juice for
a dairy-free breakfast.

100g (3½oz) quinoa flakes

30g (1oz) sunflower seeds

60ml (2fl oz) clear honey

1 tablespoon cider vinegar

2 tablespoons sunflower oil

4 teaspoons cocoa powder

pinch of salt

80g (3oz) gluten-free cornflakes

50g (2oz) gluten-free plain
puffed rice

100g (3½oz) raisins

Preheat the oven to 160°C/325°F/Gas Mark 3.

Spread the quinoa flakes and sunflower seeds over a baking
sheet and bake for 30 minutes.

Meanwhile, place the honey and vinegar in a large saucepan,
stir together and bubble over a medium heat for about
5 minutes until the mixture turns a rich brown – about the
colour of a toffee apple. Remove the pan from the heat and
quickly stir in the oil, cocoa powder and salt (the oil may not
seem to mix in at first, but everything should come together as
you keep stirring). The consistency should be similar to liquid
chocolate – if the mixture becomes too stiff, put the pan back
over the heat for a few seconds.

Tip in the toasted quinoa flakes and sunflower seeds, the
cornflakes and puffed rice and stir until a mixture of flakes
and clumps is evenly coated.

Spread the granola on to a baking sheet and leave to cool
completely, then add the raisins.

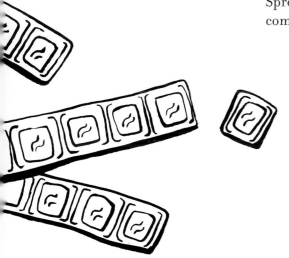

VARIATION
To make this granola
extra special, coarsely
grate 25g (1oz) chocolate
(dark or milk as you
prefer) and add to the
cooled granola with
the raisins.

Choc Crunch Granola

This chocolate-flavoured granola is perfect for those mornings
when you need a treat. It's fantastic with milk or as a topping
for yogurt, perhaps with some sliced banana as well. It will
keep for up to 2 weeks in an airtight container.

1 large banana, about 225g (7½oz)

1 dessert apple, about 100g (3½oz), cored

75g (3oz) rice flour

100g (3½oz) soft dried figs

25g (1oz) pitted prunes

2 tablespoons sunflower oil

1 teaspoon gluten-free baking powder

25g (1oz) unsweetened desiccated coconut

35g (1oz) pumpkin seeds

Preheat the oven to 160°C/325°F/Gas Mark 3.

Place the banana, apple, rice flour, figs, prunes, oil and baking powder in a food processor or blender and blend until the apple is minced into small pieces and the mixture is thick but not too chunky.

Alternatively, grate the apple, mash the banana and finely dice the figs and prunes, then mix together in a bowl. Stir in the rice flour, oil and baking powder.

Add the coconut and pumpkin seeds and mix together well. Tip into a large loaf tin, smoothing the surface with the back of a spoon.

Bake for 30 minutes until cooked through and crispy on top. Leave to cool in the tin before cutting into slices.

Figgy Fruit Bars

These bars are packed with all manner of good things and have no added sugar, making them perfect for breakfast or as a snack when you're on the go. They'll keep for up to 3 days in an airtight container.

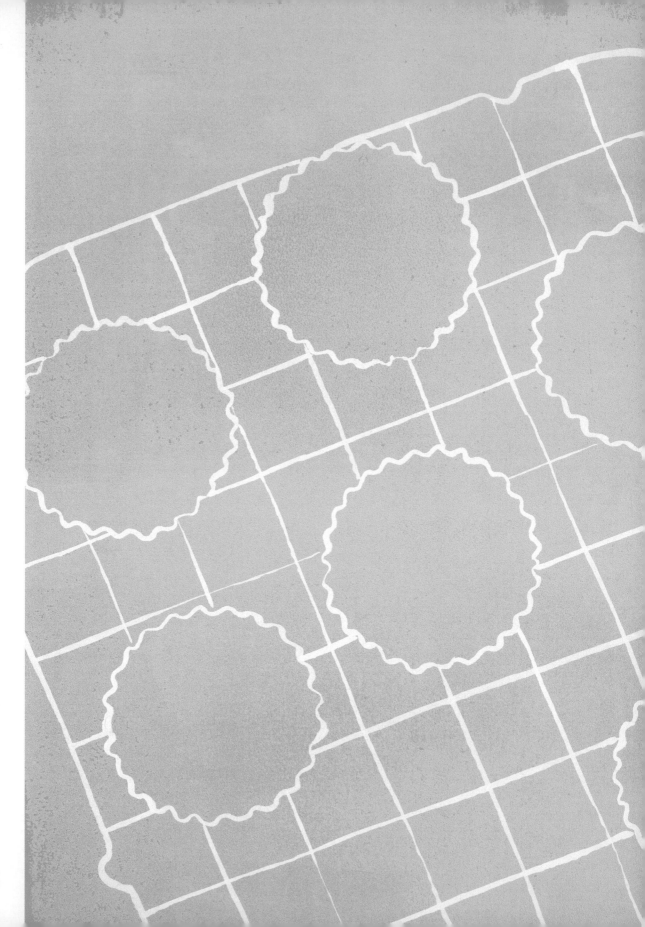

SMALL CAKES
& BISCUITS

MAKES 12

1 quantity gluten-free Sweet
Shortcrust Pastry (see page 167)

cornflour, for dusting

50g (2oz) sour cherry jam,
such as Morello

25g (1oz) unsalted butter

40g (1½oz) soft light brown sugar

25g (1oz) ground almonds

25g (1oz) brown rice flour

1 egg, lightly beaten

¼ teaspoon almond extract

2 tablespoons flaked almonds

Preheat the oven to 180°C/350°F/Gas Mark 4.

Roll out the pastry to about 3mm (⅛ inch) thick on a work surface dusted with cornflour. Stamp out 12 rounds using a fluted pastry cutter a little larger than the sections of a 12-hole tart tin. Press the pastry rounds into the tin sections, then spoon ½ teaspoon of the jam into each pastry case.

Melt the butter in a small saucepan, then stir in all the remaining ingredients except the flaked almonds. Spoon the mixture evenly over the tarts, taking care to ensure the jam is completely covered to prevent it oozing out during cooking.

Sprinkle ½ teaspoon of the flaked almonds over each tart. Bake for 20–25 minutes until golden brown and the pastry is cooked through. Leave to cool in the tin before serving.

VARIATION
Substitute the cherry jam with apricot or raspberry to give a different slant to this recipe.

Cherry Frangipane Tarts

These dinky tarts have soft domes of golden-brown almond frangipane that reveal a sour cherry jam centre. Use a fluted pastry cutter for a professional look.

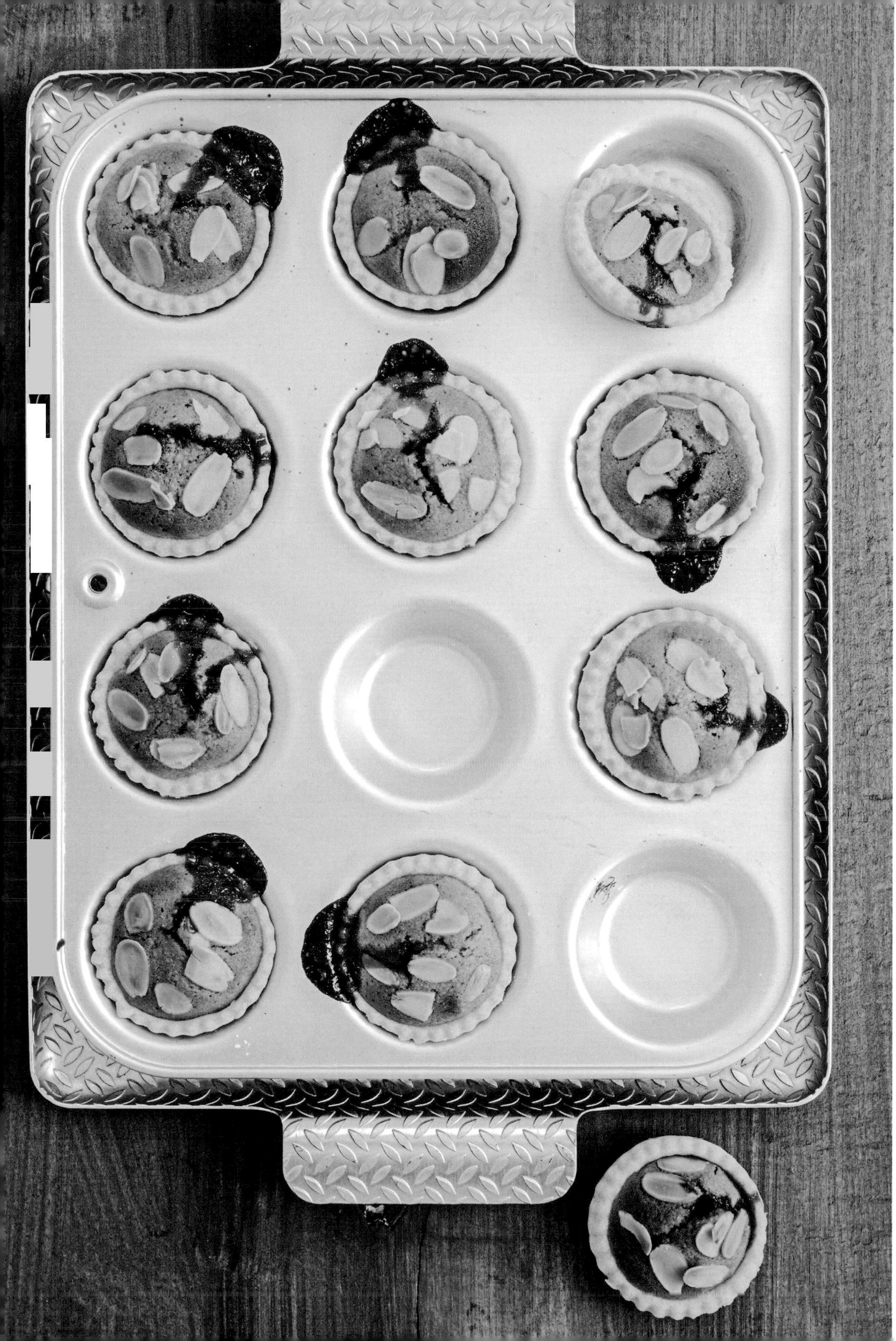

1 quantity gluten-free Sweet
Shortcrust Pastry (see page 167)

cornflour, for dusting

200g (7oz) strawberry jam

Preheat the oven to 180°C/350°F/Gas Mark 4.

Roll out the pastry to about 3mm (⅛ inch) thick on a work surface dusted with cornflour. Stamp out 18 rounds using a pastry cutter a little larger than the sections of a 12-hole tart tin. Press the pastry rounds into the sections of 2 x 12-hole tart tins, ensuring there are no holes or cracks in the pastry for the jam to seep through.

Spoon 1 teaspoon of the jam into each pastry case and bake for 30 minutes until the pastry is golden and cooked through. Transfer to a wire rack to cool – don't be tempted to eat these tarts straight from the oven because the jam will be very hot!

VARIATION

I've specified strawberry jam, but other favourite jammy fillings are raspberry, blackcurrant, blueberry or apricot.

Jam Tarts

Jam tarts are great as a way of using up excess pastry, as a fun project for the kids or just because they taste fantastic! If you're making them with scraps of pastry, the rule of thumb is 1 teaspoon of jam per tart – any more and the jam is likely to boil over and ooze all over the tray, which is not only messy, but also makes it virtually impossible to extract the tarts whole.

150g (5oz) Gluten-free Plain
White Flour Blend (see page 164)

50g (2oz) ground almonds

150g (5oz) granulated sugar

125ml (4fl oz) sunflower oil

3 eggs

2 teaspoons vanilla extract

pinch of salt

225g (7½oz) fresh blueberries

1 teaspoon cornflour

1 tablespoon gluten-free baking
powder

Preheat the oven to 160°C/325°F/Gas Mark 3.
Line a 12-hole muffin tin with paper muffin cases.

Place the flour blend, ground almonds, sugar, oil, eggs,
vanilla extract and salt in a food processor and blend for
30 seconds to form a thick batter. Alternatively, whisk
together in a bowl for 1 minute using a hand-held electric
whisk. Leave the mixture to stand for 15 minutes.

Meanwhile, toss the blueberries in the cornflour until
lightly covered (this helps to stop the blueberries sinking
to the bottom of the muffins during cooking).

Add the baking powder to the muffin mixture and
blend briefly until combined. Add the blueberries and stir
briefly (the blueberries don't need to be completely coated
with batter).

Divide the mixture evenly among the muffin cases and
bake for 30 minutes until risen and golden. Leave to cool
in the tin.

Blueberry Muffins

These moist and airy muffins are studded with gooey blueberries
and are best eaten still slightly warm from the oven. They keep
well for a couple of days, too (if there are any left!). Incidentally,
my experiments have revealed that the movement of the blueberries
during cooking is partly related to the size and shape of your
muffin cases. If you find your blueberries are sinking to the bottom,
just place the dusted blueberries on the top of the batter in the
muffin cases before you bake, rather than folding them in.
Bigger blueberries are also less likely to sink.

225g (7½oz) Gluten-free Plain White Flour Blend (see page 164)

150g (5oz) granulated sugar

180ml (6fl oz) milk

125ml (4fl oz) sunflower oil

3 eggs

grated rind of 2 large unwaxed oranges, plus extra to decorate

1 teaspoon vanilla extract

pinch of salt

20g (¾oz) poppy seeds

1 tablespoon gluten-free baking powder

Icing

100g (3½oz) icing sugar, sifted

2½ teaspoons orange juice

Preheat the oven to 160°C/325°F/Gas Mark 3. Line a 12-hole muffin tin with paper muffin cases.

Place the flour blend, sugar, milk, oil, eggs, orange rind, vanilla extract and salt in a food processor and blend for 30 seconds to form a batter. Alternatively, whisk together in a bowl for 1 minute using a hand-held electric whisk. Leave the mixture to stand for 20 minutes.

Add the poppy seeds and baking powder to the muffin mixture and blend briefly until just combined. The mixture will be runny, but this is fine.

Pour the mixture evenly into the muffin cases and bake for 20 minutes until slightly golden. Leave to cool in the tin.

To make the icing, mix together the icing sugar and orange juice in a bowl, then place a dollop on the top of each muffin. Grate a little orange rind over each muffin to decorate.

VARIATION

You can make a dairy-free version of this recipe by using soya milk in place of the milk.

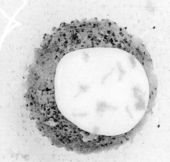

Orange Poppy Seed Muffins

These are the lightest, fluffiest muffins ever, with a lovely orange flavour and topped with a zingy citrus icing. The poppy seeds not only add an interesting texture to the muffins, they provide valuable fibre as well.

75g (3oz) Gluten-free Plain White
Flour Blend (see page 164)

60ml (2fl oz) natural yogurt

70g (2½oz) granulated sugar

12g (½oz) cocoa powder

2 eggs

75g (3oz) unsalted butter, melted

1 teaspoon gluten-free
baking powder

Chocolate icing

225g (7½oz) icing sugar, sifted

2 teaspoons cocoa powder

2 tablespoons water

Creamy vanilla frosting

125g (4oz) unsalted butter, softened

150g (5oz) condensed milk

150g (5oz) icing sugar, sifted

1 teaspoon vanilla extract

Preheat the oven to 160°C/325°F/Gas Mark 3. Line a 12-hole bun tray with paper cake cases.

Place the flour blend, yogurt, sugar, cocoa powder and eggs in a food processor. Add the melted butter and blend for 1 minute to form a batter. Alternatively, whisk together in a large bowl until well mixed. Leave the mixture to stand for 20 minutes.

Whisk the baking powder into the cake mixture, then divide evenly among the cake cases. Bake for 15 minutes until the cakes are just cooked through and a skewer inserted into the centres comes out clean. To keep the cakes moist, leave to cool in the tin under a clean tea towel.

To make the chocolate icing, mix together the ingredients in a bowl until smooth and thick, adding an extra ½ teaspoon water at a time if necessary – the icing should be thick enough that it can be spread on to the cakes without running down the sides.

To make the vanilla frosting, whisk together all the ingredients in a large bowl until well combined. Cover and chill for 30 minutes. Swirl or pipe the frosting on to your cakes as preferred, then chill the finished cakes until required.

Chocolate Cupcakes

This easy recipe gives light and delicious results every time. Even better, these moist little cakes will keep for a couple of days, so if necessary you can make them the day before you need them. To quickly upgrade your cupcakes from ordinary to ooh-la-la, top them with Chocolate Icing or Creamy Vanilla Frosting, and decorate with glacé cherries, chocolate chips or gluten-free sugar sprinkles.

175g (6oz) unsalted butter, melted, plus extra for greasing

300g (10oz) brown rice flour

150g (5oz) soft light brown sugar

100g (3½oz) granulated sugar

2 teaspoons vanilla extract

1 egg

60g (2oz) hazelnuts, chopped

120g (4oz) milk chocolate chips

Pour the melted butter into a food processor, add the rice flour, sugars, vanilla extract and egg and blend for 1 minute to form a fairly stiff, pale brown dough. Leave to rest for 30 minutes to allow the rice flour to soften up and lose its grittiness.

Preheat the oven to 170°C/340°F/Gas Mark 3½. Lightly grease 2 baking sheets.

Scrape the cookie dough into a bowl and mix in the hazelnuts and chocolate chips. Place dessertspoonfuls of the dough on to the baking sheets, spaced well apart, and flatten slightly.

Bake for 13–15 minutes until golden brown and slightly spread out. Leave to cool on the sheets. Best eaten warm.

Chewy Chocolate Chip & Hazelnut Cookies

The science behind the perfect cookie is fascinating and I've discovered that not only is a high sugar content necessary to give a gooey middle, but even minor adjustments to egg, sugar or flour quantities have a dramatic effect. It is all too easy to go from a chunky cookie with a chewy centre to one with the look and texture of a very flat cake. This makes experimentation very difficult, but with this recipe a consistently good outcome can be achieved.

50g (2oz) unsalted butter, softened, plus extra for greasing

120g (4oz) granulated sugar

100g (3½oz) Gluten-free Plain White Flour Blend (see page 164)

1½ teaspoons gluten-free ground ginger

2 teaspoons gluten-free baking powder

½ teaspoon xanthan gum

1 egg, beaten

Preheat the oven to 140°C/275°F/Gas Mark 1. Lightly grease a baking sheet with butter.

Beat together the butter and sugar in a bowl, then sift in the dry ingredients. Add half the egg (discard the rest) and whisk together until the mixture is dry and lumpy.

Knead to a dough, then break off a small piece about the size of a cherry and roll it into a ball. Flatten the ball slightly, then place it on the prepared baking sheet. Repeat with the remaining dough, spacing the balls well apart on the sheet.

Bake for 40 minutes until risen, slightly browned and hard. Transfer to a wire rack to cool.

Ginger Honeycomb Biscuits

Lightly spiced and extremely crunchy, these ginger biscuits are made using a modified version of a recipe from my mother's friend Rosemary. Their humped shape is a bit unusual, but they are possibly the nicest ginger biscuits you'll ever eat. We call them 'cave biscuits' because the honeycomb texture inside is reminiscent of limestone caverns (children are endlessly fascinated by this and require many samples to fully investigate the phenomenon). You may balk at the amount of sugar, but any reduction and these biscuits will go from cave-like to cake-like. They keep for up to 1 week in an airtight container.

50g (2oz) whole almonds

2 eggs, separated

100g (3½oz) granulated sugar

75g (3oz) ground almonds

100g (3½oz) Gluten-free Plain White Flour Blend (see page 164)

pinch of salt

sunflower oil, for greasing

Preheat the oven to 160°C/325°F/Gas Mark 3. Place the almonds on a baking sheet and roast for 5 minutes until lightly toasted.

Whisk the egg whites in a thoroughly clean bowl until stiff. Using the same whisk, whisk the egg yolks and sugar in a separate large bowl until pale and frothy. Fold in the ground almonds, flour blend, salt and egg whites until combined, then fold in the toasted nuts.

Lightly grease the baking sheet with sunflower oil. Using a spatula, spoon the mixture into 2 rectangles on the sheet, then pat out to about 8 x 15cm (3 x 6 inches). Bake for 30 minutes.

Remove the biscuit dough from the oven and leave to cool slightly. Loosen the dough from the baking sheet and cut each piece into diagonal strips using a sharp knife, then spread out the pieces on the sheet.

Reduce the oven temperature to 120°C/250°F/Gas Mark ½, return the biscotti to the oven and bake for 45–60 minutes until pale golden and completely hard. Leave to cool. Store in an airtight container.

Biscotti

An Italian favourite: try dunking these long, hard almond biscuits into coffee, tea or just cold milk. Add the grated rind of 1 large, unwaxed orange for a citrussy variation on this recipe.

150g (5oz) Gluten-free Plain White Flour Blend (see page 164), plus extra for dusting

70g (2½oz) granulated sugar

100g (3½oz) unsalted butter, softened, plus extra for greasing

grated rind of 2 unwaxed lemons

1 egg

1 teaspoon gluten-free baking powder

½ teaspoon xanthan gum

¼ teaspoon gluten-free ground cinnamon

Place all the ingredients in a bowl and stir together until the mixture forms a very soft, slightly sticky ball of dough. Cover with clingfilm and chill for 30 minutes to allow the lemon flavour to develop.

Preheat the oven to 160°C/325°F/Gas Mark 3. Grease 2 baking sheets with butter.

If you have a biscuit press, put in the dough and stamp out biscuits on to the prepared baking sheets, spacing them well apart to allow for spreading. Alternatively, turn the dough out on to a work surface dusted with flour blend and roll into a sausage about 5cm (2 inches) in diameter. Slice into rounds about 5mm (¼ inch) thick and place, spaced well apart, on the prepared baking sheets.

Bake for 18–20 minutes until golden. Using a palette knife, transfer the biscuits to a wire rack as soon as you take them out of the oven or they will stick to the sheets (pop the sheets back into the oven for a few moments if this starts to happen). Leave to cool on the wire rack. Store in an airtight container.

Lemon Biscuits

If elegance can be ascribed to a biscuit then these have it for sure: they're light and crisp with a delicate lemon flavour and a buttery moreishness. You could use a biscuit press for a professional-looking finish, but it isn't essential, because they are sure to be popular regardless.

MAKES 16

100g (3½oz) unsalted butter, plus extra for greasing

50g (2oz) icing sugar

100g (3½oz) ground almonds

100g (3½oz) brown rice flour, plus extra for dusting

¼ teaspoon xanthan gum

¼ teaspoon gluten-free baking powder

large pinch of salt

2 teaspoons caster sugar, for sprinkling

VARIATION

For a nuttier, earthier taste to your shortbread, substitute the ground almonds with ground hazelnuts.

Melt the butter in a saucepan, then add the icing sugar, ground almonds, rice flour, xanthan gum, baking powder and salt and stir together. Shape the dough into a ball, wrap in clingfilm and chill for at least 20 minutes.

Preheat the oven to 150°C/300°F/Gas Mark 2. Grease a baking sheet with butter.

Roll out the dough to about 5mm (¼ inch) thick on a work surface dusted with rice flour (if the dough cracks, warm it a little in your hands). Using a 15cm (6 inch) diameter saucer, cut out 2 large rounds, re-rolling the trimmings if necessary.

Make a frilly edge on each round by lightly pressing the flattened tip of a round-bladed knife into the dough all the way round. Cut each round into quarters, then cut the quarters in half to make 8 triangles. Prick each triangle twice with a fork to decorate. Place on the prepared baking sheet and sprinkle over the caster sugar.

Bake for 20 minutes, then reduce the oven temperature to 120°C/250°F/Gas Mark ½ and bake for a further 10 minutes until just golden. Leave to cool on the baking sheet.

The shortbread should be completely hard when cooled (if not, bake a little longer in the oven). Store in an airtight container.

Shortbread Petticoat Tails

This shortbread is rich, buttery and melt-in-the-mouth, yet also robust enough not to crumble until eaten. This traditional shape is said to mimic the contours of a flouncy underskirt, hence the name. The method used for making this shortbread is somewhat unconventional, but it's the one that works.

85ml (3fl oz) olive oil, plus extra for greasing

300g (10oz) gluten-free porridge oats

½ teaspoon salt

170ml (6fl oz) boiling water

cornflour, for dusting

Preheat the oven to 180°C/350°F/Gas Mark 4. Grease a large baking sheet with a piece of kitchen paper dipped in a little olive oil.

Place the oats, oil and salt in a heatproof bowl, pour in the measurement boiling water and stir briskly to form a thick but not sticky dough. If the dough is sticky, add a few more oats; if it's too dry, add a drop more boiling water. Leave until cool enough to handle, then knead to a smooth ball.

Roll out the dough to about 3–4mm (⅛–¼ inch) thick on a work surface dusted with cornflour. Stamp out about 25 rounds using a cookie cutter or cut into squares using a knife. Using a fish slice, transfer the rounds to the prepared baking sheet, spaced close together.

Bake for 25 minutes until pale brown at the edges and there is no trace of gooeyness in the centres. Transfer to a wire rack to cool.

VARIATION

It's easy to make different flavours – add a handful of sunflower seeds or 2 teaspoons dried rosemary to the dough before rolling it out.

Oatcakes

Gluten-free oatcakes are becoming increasingly available, but often only at a premium. It's much cheaper to make your own using gluten-free oats (and you'll probably be surprised at how easy they are to make). These will keep for up to 2 weeks in an airtight container.

MAKES 6

2 tablespoons sunflower oil,
plus extra for greasing

225g (7½oz) Gluten-free Plain
White Flour Blend (see page 164),
plus extra for dusting

125ml (4fl oz) milk

25g (1oz) granulated sugar

4 teaspoons lemon juice

1 egg, beaten

2 teaspoons gluten-free
baking powder

½ teaspoon bicarbonate of soda

Preheat the oven to 180°C/350°F/Gas Mark 4. Lightly grease
a baking sheet with sunflower oil.

Place 185g (6½oz) of the flour blend in a bowl and set aside.
Put the remaining flour blend in a saucepan with the milk, oil,
sugar and lemon juice and heat gently, stirring, until the mixture
thickens. Leave to cool for about 5 minutes, then stir in the egg.
Add half the flour in the bowl and stir together.

Add the baking powder and bicarbonate of soda to the remaining
flour in the bowl and mix together. Tip the contents into the pan
and quickly knead together thoroughly.

Turn the dough out on to a work surface dusted with a little
flour blend and gently shape it into a rough rectangle, about
3cm (1 inch) thick. Cut the rectangle into 6 pieces using a sharp
knife, then place the pieces on the prepared baking sheet and
dust with a little extra flour blend.

Bake for 15 minutes until golden. Serve warm or cold.

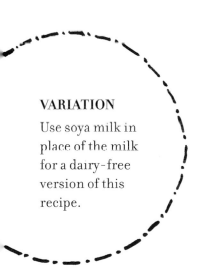

VARIATION
Use soya milk in
place of the milk
for a dairy-free
version of this
recipe.

Scones

These airy yet robust scones taste just as you'd expect. Pre-cooking
some of the flour blend ensures perfect results. Lemon juice gives
added lift, but it also means the bicarbonate of soda starts working
right away so you'll need to bake your scones as soon as you've
made the dough. Top with jam and cream for a real treat.

100g (3½oz) unsalted butter, diced, plus extra for greasing

100g (3½oz) Gluten-free Plain White Flour Blend (see page 164), plus extra for dusting

80g (3oz) potato flour

2 teaspoons gluten-free baking powder

½ teaspoon xanthan gum

150g (5oz) strong Cheddar cheese or other hard cheese, grated

1 egg, beaten

2 tablespoons water

¼ teaspoon cayenne pepper

Preheat the oven to 180°C/350°F/Gas Mark 4. Lightly grease 2 baking sheets with butter.

Mix together the flour blend, potato flour, baking powder and xanthan gum in a bowl. Add the butter and rub in with the fingertips until the mixture resembles breadcrumbs.

Reserving a couple of tablespoons of the grated cheese, stir the remainder into the flour mixture with the egg to form a soft dough.

Roll out the dough to a rectangle about 1cm (½ inch) thick on a work surface dusted with a little flour blend. Trim the edges, then cut into fingers.

Add the measurement water to the bowl that held the beaten egg and swoosh it about a bit to create an egg wash. Brush the tops of the cheese straws with the egg wash, sprinkle over the reserved cheese and a dusting of cayenne pepper.

Bake for 15 minutes until golden. Leave to cool on a wire rack before serving.

Cheese Straws

Family occasions are never complete without my sister-in-law Hannah making a huge batch of cheese straws using our friend Jane's recipe. I've modified the recipe slightly to make it gluten-free, but it's still flaky and richly cheesy. The straws will keep for a few days in an airtight container.

sunflower oil, for greasing

100g (3½oz) Gluten-free Plain White Flour Blend (see page 164), plus extra for dusting

½ teaspoon gluten-free baking powder

¼ teaspoon xanthan gum

¼ teaspoon salt, plus extra for sprinkling

1 tablespoon pure vegetable fat

85ml (3fl oz) water

Preheat the oven to 160°C/325°F/Gas Mark 3. Lightly grease a baking sheet with sunflower oil.

Place the flour blend, baking powder, xanthan gum and salt in a bowl and stir together. Add the vegetable fat and rub in with the fingertips until the mixture resembles breadcrumbs. Add the measurement water and mix together to form a smooth and very malleable dough, adding a little extra water or flour as necessary.

Roll out the dough to about 1mm (¹⁄₁₆ inch) thick on a work surface dusted with flour blend – the dough should be so thin it is almost translucent. Sprinkle with salt and gently roll over the dough so the salt is pressed in. Stamp out about 20 rounds using a 6cm (2½ inch) pastry cutter.

Transfer the rounds to the prepared baking sheet and bake for 30 minutes until very crisp (the crackers won't have browned much, but they will have an excellent 'snap'). Transfer to a wire rack to cool. Store in an airtight container.

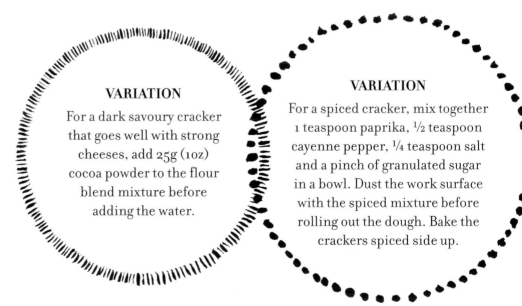

VARIATION

For a dark savoury cracker that goes well with strong cheeses, add 25g (1oz) cocoa powder to the flour blend mixture before adding the water.

VARIATION

For a spiced cracker, mix together 1 teaspoon paprika, ½ teaspoon cayenne pepper, ¼ teaspoon salt and a pinch of granulated sugar in a bowl. Dust the work surface with the spiced mixture before rolling out the dough. Bake the crackers spiced side up.

Crackers

These plain crackers, or water biscuits as they are also known, are lovely to scoop into dips or served topped with cheese or pâté. Try this basic version or go for one of my flavour variations.

4 slices of gluten-free bread

Preheat the oven to 100°C/225°F/Gas Mark ¼.

Toast the bread on both sides until a light golden brown, then cut off the crusts.

Using a bread knife, cut each piece of toast horizontally into 2 thin sheets, then cut each sheet diagonally to form 2 triangles. Lay the triangles on a baking sheet and bake for 30 minutes until completely dried out.

Melba Toast

Melba toast is a quick and easy way of making crackers if you want something to accompany cheese or pâté, or to serve with soup. The toast will keep for up to a week in an airtight container.

INDULGENCE

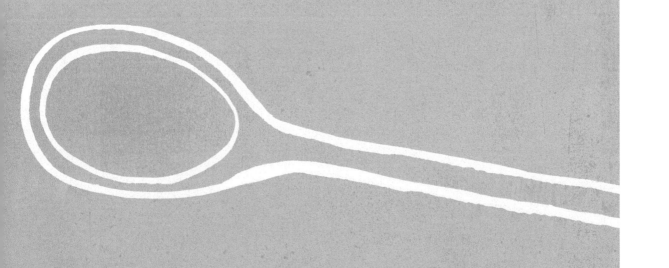

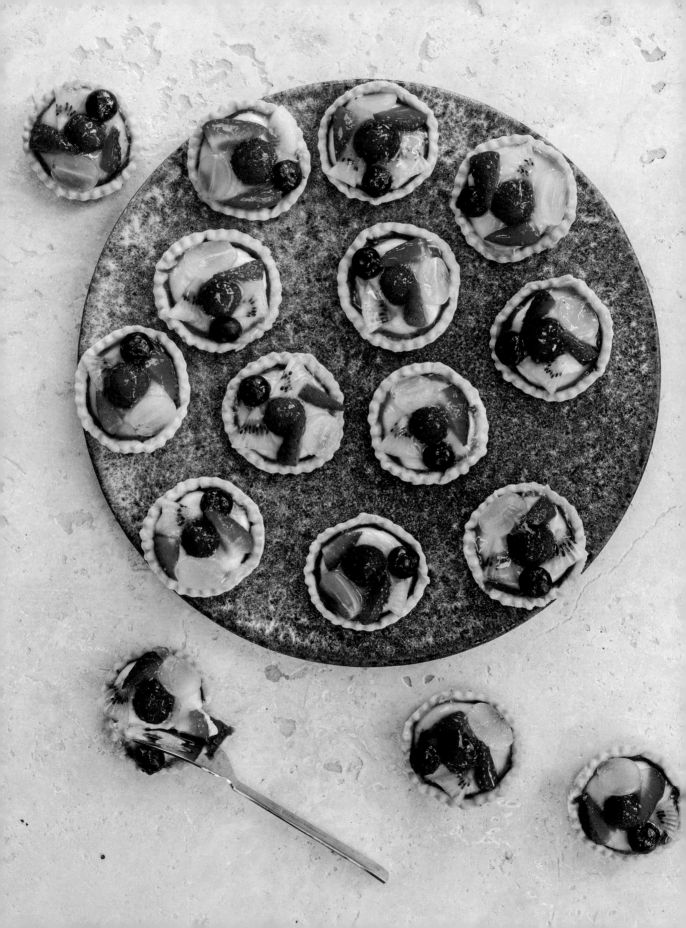

vegetable oil, for greasing

1 quantity gluten-free Rich Sweet
Shortcrust Pastry (see page 167)

cornflour, for dusting

50g (2oz) milk chocolate,
broken into pieces

18 raspberries

4 strawberries, hulled and
chopped

1 kiwifruit, peeled and cut
into small triangles

9 green grapes, halved

18 blueberries

Crème pâtissière

2 egg yolks

1 tablespoon granulated sugar

4 teaspoons cornflour

1 teaspoon vanilla extract

250ml (8fl oz) milk

Glaze

170ml (6fl oz) water

1 tablespoon granulated sugar

2 teaspoons agar flakes

2 ice cubes

Preheat the oven to 180°C/ 350°F/Gas Mark 4. Lightly grease
the sections of 2 x 12-hole tart tins with vegetable oil.

Roll out the pastry to about 2mm (⅛ inch) thick on a work surface
dusted with cornflour. Stamp out 18 circles using a fluted pastry
cutter a little larger than the tin sections. Press the pastry rounds
into the tin sections, then fill each pastry case with ceramic
baking beans. Bake for 30 minutes, until crisp and just golden.
Remove the beans and leave the tartlets to cool on a wire rack.

Melt the chocolate in a heatproof bowl set over a saucepan of
simmering water. Using a pastry brush, carefully spread the
chocolate evenly over each pastry case, then chill until set.

To make the crème pâtissière, beat together the egg yolks and
sugar in a large bowl. Whisk in the cornflour and vanilla extract.
Heat the milk until just boiling, then slowly pour it into the egg
mixture, whisking continuously. Pour into the saucepan and heat
gently, whisking continuously until it starts to thicken. Remove
the pan from the heat and leave to cool, whisking occasionally
to prevent a skin from forming.

When the crème pâtissière is at room temperature, spoon
a heaped teaspoonful into each case and top with the fruit. Chill
for 30 minutes. Place a saucer in the refrigerator at the same time.

To make the glaze, put the measurement water and sugar into a
saucepan over a medium heat. Add the agar flakes and simmer
for about 10 minutes, stirring occasionally, until completely
dissolved. Add an ice cube and stir until it melts. Break up the
second ice cube and add small pieces at a time until the agar
liquid starts to thicken – a teaspoonful dropped on to the chilled
saucer should set almost immediately.

Quickly spoon 1–2 teaspoons of the glaze over the fruit in each
tart. Chill the tarts for 30 minutes before serving.

Glazed Fruit Tartlets

The combination of delicate pastry, crème pâtissière and
jewel-like fruit appeals to me. Although time-consuming
to make, these sophisticated little tarts are worth it.

1 quantity gluten-free Rich Sweet Shortcrust Pastry (see page 167)

cornflour, for dusting

2 unwaxed lemons

100g (3½oz) icing sugar, plus extra for dusting

250ml (8fl oz) double cream

1 egg, beaten

Preheat the oven to 180°C/350°F/Gas Mark 4.

Roll out the pastry to about 4mm (¼ inch) thick on a work surface dusted with cornflour. Line a 20cm (8 inch) tart tin with the pastry and trim any excess using a sharp knife. Line the case with foil or baking paper, then fill with dried beans or ceramic baking beans. Bake for 30 minutes until golden. Remove the paper and beans and leave to cool.

Meanwhile, make the filling. Cut 4 strips of rind from 1 lemon using a potato peeler, then squeeze the juice from both lemons. Place about 125ml (4fl oz) of the juice, the lemon rind and icing sugar in a saucepan and heat, stirring, until boiling. Remove the rind. In a separate pan, heat the cream until boiling.

Remove the cream from the heat and quickly whisk in the lemon mixture. Continue whisking for about 1 minute, then leave to cool for about 5 minutes. Whisk in the egg. Place the pan over a medium heat and cook, whisking continuously, until the mixture boils. Remove the pan from the heat and leave to cool slightly.

When the mixture is the consistency of yogurt, whisk for about 10 seconds, then pour into the pastry case. Chill for at least 4 hours, or overnight, until set. Dust with a little icing sugar before serving.

Lemon Tart

This tart is based on the classic French tarte au citron, famous for its silky smooth, tangy lemon filling. Unlike most recipes, the filling does not need to be cooked in the oven, but does require at least 4 hours to set. The tart will keep for a couple of days.

1 quantity gluten-free Rich Sweet Shortcrust Pastry (see page 167)

cornflour, for dusting

150g (5oz) pecan halves

160g (5½oz) sof dark brown sugar

2 tablespoons maple syrup

100g (3½oz) unsalted butter

¼ teaspoon salt

3 eggs

Preheat the oven to 180°C/350°F/Gas Mark 4.

Roll out the pastry to about 4mm (¼ inch) thick on a work surface dusted with cornflour. Line a 20cm (8 inch) tart tin with the pastry and trim any excess using a sharp knife. Spread the nuts evenly over the case.

Place the sugar, syrup, butter and salt in a saucepan and gently heat until the mixture forms a caramel. Leave to bubble for a couple of minutes, then remove the pan from the heat. Leave to cool for about 5 minutes.

Meanwhile, using a fork, beat together the eggs in a large bowl until just mixed (if you whisk there is a risk of creating foamy eggs, which don't make for a pleasant end result). Gradually pour in the cooled caramel, beating continuously with the fork, then pour into the case. Bake for 30 minutes until the filling has set and the pastry is golden.

Pecan Pie

This is a classic tart from the southern USA, packed with pecan nuts in a toffee-like base. My recipe is less sweet than many others as I prefer a nutty taste unburdened by tooth-aching sugariness, but if you like it sweeter, use 200g (7oz) soft dark brown sugar. Pecan pie is a delicious dessert at any time of year. Try it hot or cold, with cream.

300g (10oz) peeled pumpkin flesh, chopped

1 quantity gluten-free Rich Sweet Shortcrust Pastry (see page 167)

cornflour, for dusting

100g (3½oz) unsalted butter, melted

80g (3oz) soft dark brown sugar

85ml (3fl oz) natural yogurt

60ml (2fl oz) whisky

2 teaspoons cornflour

¼ teaspoon gluten-free ground cinnamon

pinch of salt

3 eggs, separated

Preheat the oven to 180°C/350°F/Gas Mark 4.

Place the pumpkin in a saucepan, add enough water to cover and bring to the boil, then cook for 15 inutes until tender.

Meanwhile, roll out the pastry to about 3mm (⅛ inch) thick on a work surface dusted with cornflour. Line a 25cm (10 inch) loose-bottomed tart tin with the pastry and trim any excess using a sharp knife.

Drain the pumpkin, then place in a food processor or blender with the remaining ingredients except the eggs and blend until completely smooth. Add the egg yolks and combine.

Whisk the egg whites in a thoroughly clean large bowl until they form soft peaks. Pour the pumpkin mixture down the side of the bowl, then carefully fold together. Tip the mixture into the prepared pastry case and bake for about 45 minutes until the pie is puffy and browned. It will collapse a little as it cools, but this is normal.

Pumpkin Pie

This American classic is inspired by an old Pennsylvania Dutch recipe and combines the earthiness of whisky, the toffee flavours of brown sugar and the slight acidity of yogurt to make an irresistible dessert that will fill your kitchen with mouthwatering aromas. If pumpkin is out of season, butternut squash works just as well. Serve hot or cold, with a little cream or ice cream.

125g (4oz) gluten-free sweet plain hard biscuits

150g (5oz) unsalted butter

300g (10oz) condensed milk

125ml (4fl oz) soured cream or crème fraîche

3 bananas, sliced

25g (1oz) dark chocolate, grated

Place the biscuits in a sealed plastic food bag and bash with a rolling pin to form crumbs. Alternatively, blitz them in a food processor. Melt 50g (2oz) of the butter in a small saucepan, then stir in the biscuit crumbs until well combined.

Tip the crumbs into a deep 20cm (8 inch) loose-bottomed tart tin and smooth the mixture level using the back of a metal tablespoon. Chill for at least 1 hour until firm.

To make the toffee, melt the remaining butter in a saucepan over a medium heat, then gradually pour in the condensed milk, whisking continuously (condensed milk can burn very easily and if it does you'll end up with dark flecks in your toffee, so keep stirring). Bring the mixture to the boil, then remove the pan from the heat and pour on to the biscuit base. Chill for at least 1 hour.

Spread the soured cream or crème fraîche over the toffee layer, then arrange the banana slices over the top. Sprinkle with the grated chocolate and serve.

Banoffee Pie

Banoffee pie is surprisingly simple to make, though it is very indulgent, which is why I offset the sweetness with a soured cream topping. This dessert never fails to delight – provided your guests like bananas. If you suddenly discover you have a banana-hater, then the crunchy base and toffee topping also taste fantastic combined with other fruit, such as blueberries, passion fruits or – my personal favourite – a couple of crisp grated apples.

50g (2oz) unsalted butter, plus extra for greasing

150g (5oz) plain dark chocolate, broken into pieces

6 eggs, separated

70g (2½oz) granulated sugar

100g (3½oz) Gluten-free Plain White Flour Blend (see page 164)

50g (2oz) ground almonds

pinch of salt

Icing

100g (3½oz) plain dark chocolate, broken into pieces

100g (3½oz) unsalted butter

250ml (8fl oz) condensed milk

pinch of salt

Preheat the oven to 160°C/325°F/Gas Mark 3. Lightly grease 2 x 20cm (8 inch) sandwich tins with butter.

Place the chocolate and butter in a saucepan over a very low heat and heat until the chocolate is almost completely melted, then stir the mixture and remove the pan from the heat. Set aside.

Whisk the egg whites in a thoroughly clean bowl until stiff. Using the same whisk, whisk the egg yolks and sugar in a separate large bowl until pale and thick.

Fold in the flour blend, ground almonds and salt. Carefully pour the chocolate mixture down the side of the bowl and fold in, then fold in the egg whites until combined.

Pour the cake mixture evenly into the prepared tins, then tip the tins from side to side to level the mixture. Bake for 20 minutes until a skewer inserted into the centres comes out clean (the cakes won't rise much). Leave to cool in the tins for a few minutes, then loosen the edges with a palette knife and turn out on to a wire rack. Leave to cool.

To make the icing, place all the ingredients in a saucepan and heat gently, stirring, until the mixture is dark and glossy. While still warm, spread a thick layer of icing over 1 cake. Place the second cake on top, upside down. Spread the remaining icing over the top and sides. You can make decorative designs in the icing with a fork, if you wish. Leave to set for 1 hour before serving.

Chocolate Fudge Cake

This rich chocolate cake is decadence on a plate – dense (but not heavy), moist and smothered in a thick, glossy chocolate fudge icing. It is not at all crumbly so it makes the perfect party cake: you can slice it as thin as you like, confident each piece will look perfect. The cake keeps well for a couple of days.

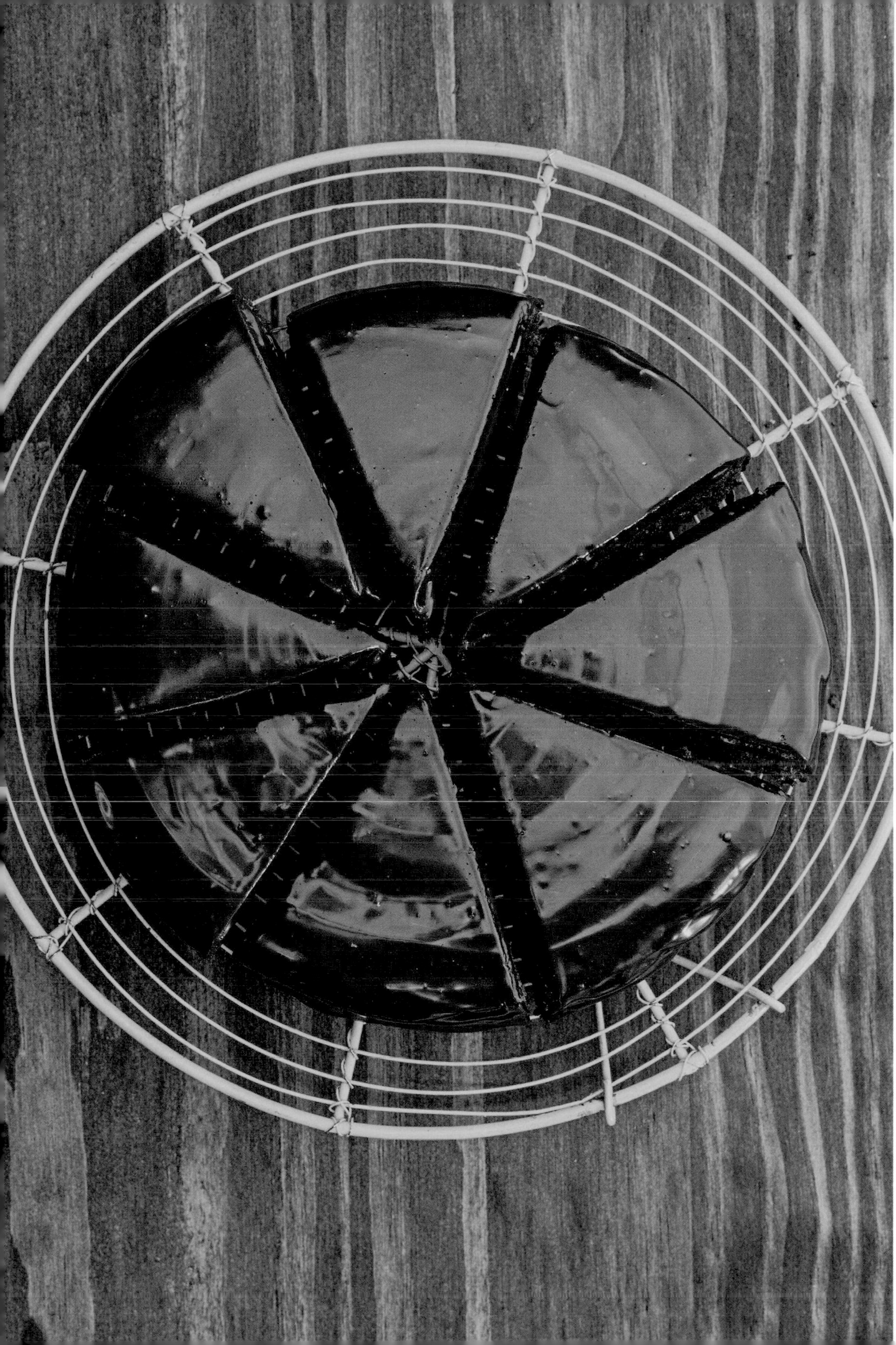

200g (7oz) seedless raisins or sultanas

50g (2oz) dried apricots, finely chopped

60ml (2fl oz) black tea

60ml (2fl oz) orange juice

100g (3½oz) unsalted butter, plus extra for greasing

50g (2oz) glacé cherries, rinsed, dried and roughly chopped

2 teaspoons gluten-free mixed spice

120g (4oz) soft dark brown sugar

125g (4oz) thick-cut marmalade or apricot jam

60g (2oz) treacle

200g (7oz) buckwheat flour

100g (3½oz) ground almonds

4 teaspoons gluten-free baking powder

2 eggs, lightly beaten

¼ teaspoon salt

Place the raisins or sultanas, apricots, tea and orange juice in a bowl. Leave to soak overnight.

The next day, preheat the oven to 120°C/250°F/Gas Mark ½. Wrap the outside of a deep 20cm (8 inch) cake tin with a piece of nonstick baking paper folded lengthways twice to create a four-layered strip (the extra layers prevent the outside of the cake getting too dry). Grease the inside of the tin with a little butter.

Place the cherries in a small bowl, sprinkle with the mixed spice and stir together.

Melt the butter in a saucepan, then stir in the sugar, marmalade or jam and treacle. Add the buckwheat flour, ground almonds, baking powder, eggs and salt. Stir until well combined, then fold in the spiced cherries and soaked fruit.

Spoon the mixture into the prepared tin and level the top. Cover the tin with foil, then prick a few holes in the foil with a skewer. Bake for 3½ hours until well browned – do not open the oven door during the cooking time. A skewer inserted into the centre should come out clean. Leave to cool in the tin.

VARIATION
Make a dairy-free version by using dairy-free margarine instead of butter.

Rich Fruit Cake

This is a spiced fruitcake packed with raisins, apricots and cherries. For best results a little forethought is needed: the fruit should ideally soak overnight and the cake is also better if left for a day or two before it is eaten.

sunflower oil, for greasing

200g (7oz) whole hazelnuts

6 eggs, separated

160g (5½oz) icing sugar

Raspberry cream

375ml (12fl oz) whipping cream

300g (10oz) fresh raspberries

35g (1oz) icing sugar

Preheat the oven to 160°C/325°F/Gas Mark 3. Lightly grease 2 x 20cm (8 inch) sandwich tins with sunflower oil and line the bases with nonstick baking paper.

Place the hazelnuts on a baking sheet and roast for 10 minutes. Leave to cool for 5 minutes, then blitz in a food processor until the texture of coffee grinds.

Whisk the egg whites in a thoroughly clean large bowl until stiff (you should be able to hold the bowl upside down without the whites falling out). Using the same whisk, whisk the icing sugar and egg yolks in a separate bowl until pale and mousse-like. Carefully fold the yolk mixture into the egg whites, then fold in the ground hazelnuts and combine well.

Divide the mixture evenly between the tins and bake for 20 minutes until set. Leave to cool in the tins.

Meanwhile, whip the cream in a large bowl. Using a fork, mash half of the raspberries with the icing sugar in a separate bowl (reserve the best raspberries for decoration), then fold into the cream.

Turn out the cakes on to a wire rack and peel off the baking paper. Using a bread knife, cut each cake horizontally into 2 even layers.

To assemble, place a layer of cake on a large, flat serving dish and spread over a 1cm (½ inch) thick layer of the raspberry cream using a spatula. Repeat with the remaining cakes and cream. Decorate with the reserved raspberries and eat on the same day.

Raspberry Hazelnut Gateau

This delicious gateau has voluptuous raspberry-flavoured cream billowing across four layers of moist hazelnut sponge. But it's not just pretty — it's also pretty simple to make.

200g (7oz) gluten-free amaretti biscuits, broken into small pieces

125ml (4fl oz) strong coffee or espresso, cooled

60ml (2fl oz) brandy

2 eggs, separated

1 tablespoon soft dark brown sugar

2 teaspoons vanilla extract

300g (10oz) mascarpone

25g (1oz) milk chocolate, finely grated, to serve

Place the biscuits in a bowl, pour over the coffee and brandy and leave to soak for about 10 minutes until softened. Stir occasionally to ensure the biscuits have absorbed the liquid.

Whisk the egg whites in a thoroughly clean bowl until they form soft peaks. Using the same whisk, whisk the egg yolks, sugar and vanilla extract in a separate bowl until frothy and doubled in volume. Add the mascarpone, a little at a time, whisking until well combined. Fold in the egg whites.

Divide the soaked amaretti mixture among dessert glasses or wine glasses (the more decorative, the better), then top with the mascarpone mixture and chill for at least 30 minutes.

To serve, top with the grated chocolate.

Tiramisu

Coffee-soaked amaretti biscuits lend an unusual twist to this tiramisu, though it does contain alcohol and raw egg so it's not suitable for everyone. This dessert needs to be eaten the day it is made.

SERVES 6

sunflower oil, for greasing

2 eggs, separated

50g (2oz) granulated sugar

35g (1oz) brown rice flour

Filling

5 sheets of leaf gelatine

125ml (4fl oz) dairy-free mango smoothie

250ml (8fl oz) whipping cream

50g (2oz) icing sugar

Topping

1 sheet of leaf gelatine

60ml (2fl oz) dairy-free mango smoothie

2 large passion fruits, seeds and juice

Preheat the oven to 180°C/350°F/Gas Mark 4. Grease the sides of a deep 18cm (7 inch) springform cake tin with sunflower oil and line the base with nonstick baking paper.

Whisk the egg whites in a clean bowl until they form soft peaks. Whisk the egg yolks and sugar in a separate large bowl until pale and thick. Sift the rice flour into the yolk mixture and fold in with a metal spoon, then fold in the whites, taking care to retain as much air as possible.

Pour the mixture into the prepared cake tin and bake for about 20 minutes until golden. Leave to cool in the tin.

Meanwhile, to make the filling, soak the gelatine in a bowl of cold water for 5 minutes until soft. Drain, then add to the mango smoothie and heat gently (I do this in a microwave) until the gelatine dissolves. Stir, then leave to stand for about 20 minutes until it reaches room temperature.

Gently run a knife round the sides of the cake tin, then turn the sponge out on to a large plate. Clean the tin, then lightly grease the sides with sunflower oil. Place the sponge upside down in the tin and carefully remove the baking paper.

Whip the cream and icing sugar in a bowl until firm, then fold in the gelatine mixture. Pour the mixture into the tin and smooth the top using a spatula. Chill for about 2 hours.

To make the topping, soak the gelatine in cold water for 5 minutes until soft. Drain, then add to the mango smoothie and heat gently until the gelatine dissolves. Leave to stand for about 20 minutes.

Stir the passion fruit pulp into the gelatine mixture, then pour into the tin, completely covering the fruit cream. Chill for 1 hour.

To serve, carefully run a palette knife round the inside of the tin to loosen the cake, then transfer to a serving dish.

Passion Fruit Mousse Cake

Eating this cake is like biting into a tropical cloud. If you want to be really fancy, you can turn the cake into petits fours: use an oiled cookie cutter to punch out as many pieces as you can.

SERVES 6

3 egg whites

½ teaspoon gluten-free
baking powder

160g (5½oz) soft light
brown sugar

30g (1oz) flaked almonds

60g (2oz) gluten-free cornflakes

To serve

250ml (8fl oz) whipping cream

1 kiwifruit, peeled and thinly
sliced

175g (6oz) green seedless grapes

Preheat the oven to 160°C/325°F/Gas Mark 3. Line a
20cm (8 inch) tart tin with nonstick baking paper.

Whisk together the egg whites and baking powder in a
thoroughly clean bowl until very stiff (you should be able to
hold the bowl upside down without the whites falling out).
Gradually whisk in the sugar, a little at a time. Set aside.

Toast the almonds in a small dry frying pan over a medium-high
heat for a few minutes until golden brown, stirring frequently
to prevent them burning.

Using a food mixer or pestle and mortar, crush the cornflakes
into crumbs. Fold the crumbs and toasted almonds into the
meringue mixture.

Pour the mixture into the prepared tin and bake for 40 minutes
until puffy and slightly browned (the puffiness will disappear as
the meringue cools, but this is normal). Remove from the oven
and leave to cool.

Remove the cooled meringue from the tin and place on a
serving plate. Whip the cream until firm, then spread over the
meringue base. Arrange the kiwi slices around the edge of the
cream, then pile the grapes in the centre. Serve immediately.

Almond Meringue

This recipe is adapted from one given to me by my Auntie Maureen,
who frequently makes it for her guests (including me!). It's a cross
between a pavlova and an almond tart, with the juicy green fruit
making the perfect contrast to the sweet nutty, chewy base.

SERVES 6

350g (11½oz) carrots,
peeled and sliced

50g (2oz) dried pitted dates

150g (5oz) golden syrup

80g (3oz) soft dark brown sugar

1 egg

150g (5oz) brown rice flour

1 teaspoon bicarbonate of soda

¼ teaspoon salt

110g (4oz) cold pure vegetable fat

Sauce

250ml (8fl oz) single cream

110g (3½oz) unsalted butter

55g (2oz) soft dark brown sugar

pinch of salt

Cook the carrots in a saucepan of boiling water until soft. Drain, then place in a food processor with the dates, golden syrup, sugar and egg and blend until smooth. Add the rice flour, bicarbonate of soda, salt and vegetable fat and pulse for 5–10 seconds until the flour is mixed in and the fat is minced into small pieces.

Pour the mixture into a 1.5 litre (2½ pint) pudding basin. Cover the pudding basin with a piece of pleated foil and secure with cook's string or an elastic band.

Place an upturned heatproof saucer in the bottom of a stockpot or large, heavy-based saucepan. Place the pudding on the saucer, then pour in water until it comes about one-third up the side of the pudding basin. Cover with a lid and bring to the boil, then reduce the heat and simmer for 3½ hours until the pudding is cooked through.

To make the sauce, place all the ingredients in a saucepan and heat gently until the sugar has dissolved, then bring to the boil and cook until thickened.

Run a knife round the edge of the basin to loosen the pudding, then turn it out on to a plate. Pour over the hot sauce and serve.

If not required immediately, the cooked pudding will keep in the refrigerator for a couple of days. To reheat, cook the pudding as above for 1 hour or remove the foil, loosely place a saucer on top of the basin and microwave on medium-high for about 5 minutes until the pudding is piping hot.

Sticky Toffee Pudding

I've drawn on traditional techniques to create this steamed syrup and date sponge – carrots help to create its light texture. The sponge is served with a toffee sauce so heavenly it would make angels weep.

SERVES 6

25g (1oz) unsalted butter,
plus extra for greasing

100g (3½oz) brown rice flour

100g (3½oz) granulated sugar

125ml (4fl oz) milk

1 teaspoon vanilla extract

55g (2oz) cornflour

1 tablespoon cocoa powder

2 teaspoons gluten-free
baking powder

1 egg, lightly beaten

Sauce

110g (3½oz) soft dark brown sugar

25g (1oz) cocoa powder

250ml (8fl oz) boiling water

170ml (6fl oz) milk

Preheat the oven to 170°C/340°F/Gas Mark 3½.
Grease a 1.75 litre (3 pint) pudding basin with butter.

Place the rice flour, sugar, butter, milk and vanilla extract
in a saucepan and whisk together over a medium-low heat
until the butter has melted and the mixture has thickened
to form a paste.

Remove the pan from the heat and whisk in the cornflour,
cocoa powder, baking powder and egg. Spoon the mixture
into the prepared pudding basin.

For the sauce, sprinkle the brown sugar and cocoa powder
over the mixture, then pour on the measurement boiling
water and milk. Place on a baking sheet and bake for
45–50 minutes until risen and the sauce has a custard-
like consistency.

Remove from the oven and leave to cool for 5–10 minutes.
Carefully invert on to a lipped plate or shallow bowl and
serve immediately.

Hot Chocolate Pudding

A touch of oven magic turns a large dollop of cake mixture
topped with boiling water into a mouthwatering chocolate
sponge with a pool of rich chocolate sauce underneath. Ideally,
this dessert should be served as it emerges from the oven,
so aim to make it about an hour before you want it.
Delicious with cream or ice cream.

MAKES 12

sunflower oil, for greasing

100g (3½oz) dark chocolate, broken into pieces

100g (3½oz) milk chocolate, broken into pieces

85ml (3fl oz) water

250ml (8fl oz) whipping cream

Choux pastry

50g (2oz) unsalted butter

170ml (6fl oz) water

110g (3½oz) cornflour

2 eggs, beaten

Preheat the oven to 180°C/350°F/Gas Mark 4. Lightly oil a baking sheet with sunflower oil. Place it under cold running water to wet the surface, then tip away any excess water.

To make the choux pastry, heat the butter and measurement water in a saucepan until boiling. Remove the pan from the heat and tip the contents into a blender. Add the cornflour and blend until smooth. Leave to cool for a few minutes, then add the eggs and blend until the mixture is glossy and thick.

Using a tablespoon, place 12 equal-sized dollops, spaced well apart, on the prepared baking sheet. Bake for 10 minutes, then increase the oven temperature to 200°C/400°F/Gas Mark 6 and cook for a further 15–20 minutes until golden brown. Using a skewer, make a small hole in the side of each choux bun to release the steam, then transfer to a wire rack to cool.

To serve, heat the chocolate and measurement water in a saucepan over a gentle heat until the chocolate melts. Stir to combine, then remove from the heat. Whip the cream until stiff peaks form. Cut each profiterole in half and spoon in a generous quantity of cream, then sandwich them back together. Arrange the profiteroles in separate bowls or on one large dish, drizzle over the chocolate sauce and serve.

Profiteroles

Just about everyone loves profiteroles drizzled with chocolate sauce. This gluten-free version is surprisingly easy provided you follow my slightly unorthodox method. The plain pastry buns will keep for a day or two, but the filling and sauce should only be added when the dessert is ready to serve.

SERVES 6

sunflower oil, for greasing

6 eggs, separated

120g (4oz) granulated sugar

50g (2oz) cocoa powder

2 x 400g (13oz) cans pitted
Morello cherries in juice

1 tablespoon rum

250ml (8fl oz) whipping cream

2 teaspoons icing sugar

25g (1oz) plain dark chocolate,
to decorate

Preheat the oven to 160°C/325°F/Gas Mark 3. Grease
2 x 20cm (8 inch) sandwich tins with sunflower oil and
line with nonstick baking paper.

Whisk the egg whites in a thoroughly clean bowl until they
form soft peaks. Using the same whisk, whisk the egg yolks
and sugar in a separate large bowl until pale and thick. Sift in
the cocoa powder and fold in, then carefully fold in the whites.

Divide the mixture evenly between the prepared tins,
smoothing the tops using a palette knife or spatula. Bake
for 15–20 minutes until just cooked. Leave to cool in the tins
for about 15 minutes. Run a palette knife round the edge to
loosen them, then turn out on to a wire rack and peel off the
baking paper. Leave to cool completely.

Drain the cherries, reserving 2 tablespoons of the juice and
a handful of whole cherries for decoration. Roughly chop the
remaining cherries. Mix together the reserved cherry juice
and the rum.

Whip the cream and icing sugar until it forms soft peaks.

Spoon the cherry juice over 1 cake, then neatly spread
over one-third of the cream using a palette knife. Top with
the chopped cherries, then sandwich together with the
remaining cake. Spread the remaining cream over the sides
and top of the cake.

To make chocolate curls, run a vegetable peeler down
the side of the block of chocolate. Use the curls and whole
cherries to decorate the top of the cake.

Chill for at least 30 minutes before serving.

Black Forest Gateau

Real Black Forest gateaux are made with cocoa powder in place
of wheat flour, making them naturally gluten-free. This recipe is
adapted from the one by Delia Smith in her *Complete Cookery
Course* – it is so tasty that I didn't feel it needed any further
messing about. The gateau should be eaten the day it is made.

Base

100g (3½oz) unsalted butter, plus extra for greasing

100g (3½oz) ground almonds

100g (3½oz) brown rice flour

35g (1oz) icing sugar

½ teaspoon xanthan gum

large pinch of salt

[handwritten note in left margin: r mik 3 (ckerry)]

Caramel

100g (3½oz) unsalted butter

½ teaspoon salt

300g (10oz) condensed milk

1 teaspoon treacle

Topping

125g (4oz) milk chocolate, broken into pieces

2 pinches of sea salt

Preheat the oven to 150°C/300°F/Gas Mark 2. Lightly grease a 20cm (8 inch) square loose-bottomed brownie tin with butter.

To make the base, melt the butter in a saucepan, then stir in the remaining ingredients. Using the back of a metal spoon, press the mixture into the tin and smooth the surface. Prick all over with a fork and bake for 25 minutes. Leave to cool in the tin.

To make the caramel, melt the butter in a saucepan over a medium heat, add the salt and gradually pour in the condensed milk. Increase the heat to medium-high and stir continuously until the mixture starts to boil. Stir briskly for a few minutes until the mixture is thick and golden brown. Remove the pan from the heat and stir in the treacle. Stir well again and immediately pour over the cooled shortbread and smooth out using a spatula. Set aside to cool completely.

Melt the chocolate in a small heatproof bowl set over a pan of simmering water, making sure the base of the bowl does not touch the water. Alternatively, melt in a microwave on a low heat. Spread the chocolate evenly across the caramel, then sprinkle over the sea salt and leave to set.

Cut into 16 squares with a sharp knife, then carefully remove from the tin.

Salted Caramel Millionaire's Shortbread

For a real treat, indulge in these chocolate-topped shortbread squares with an irresistible layer of soft and chewy salted caramel in the centre.

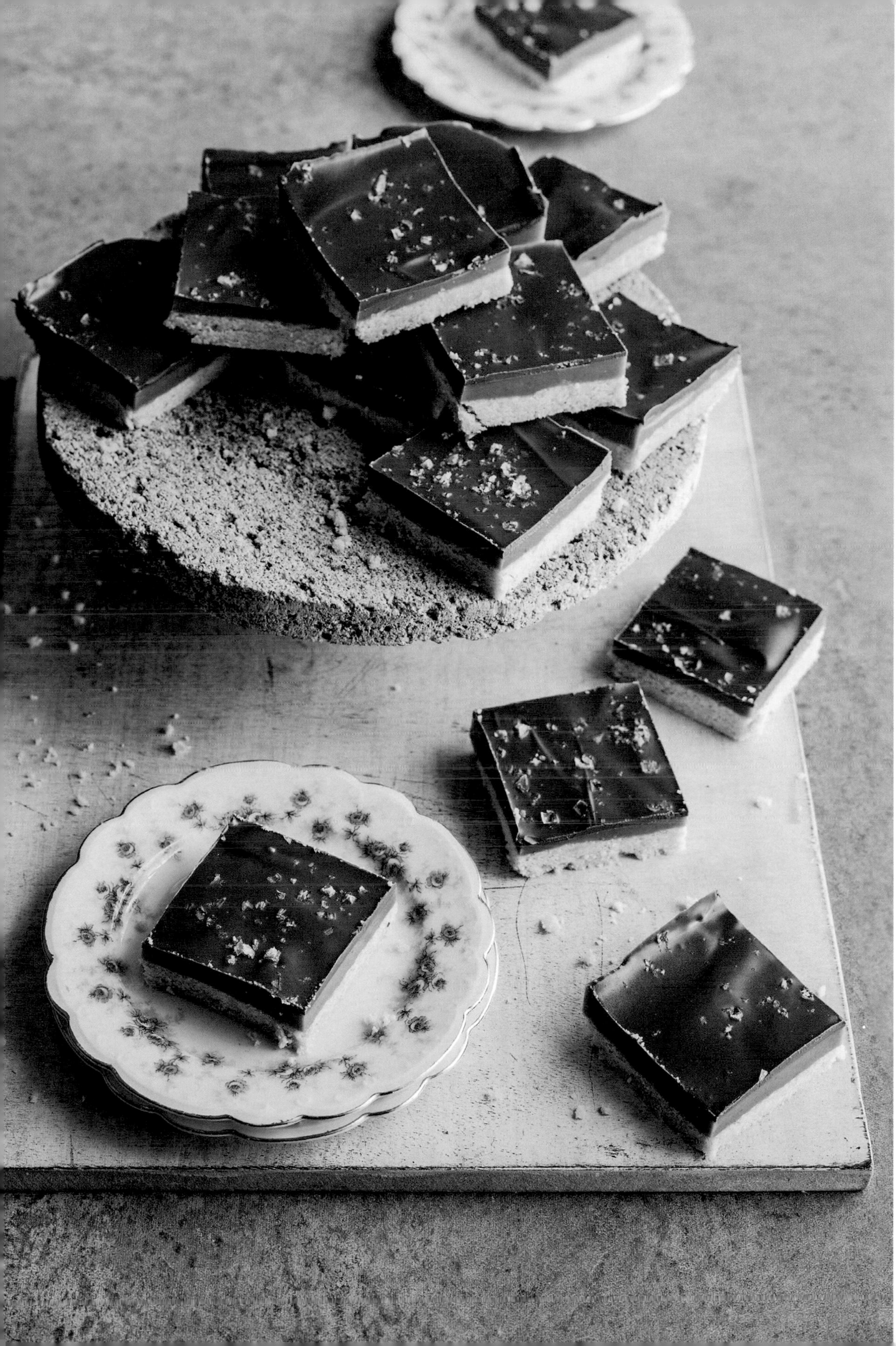

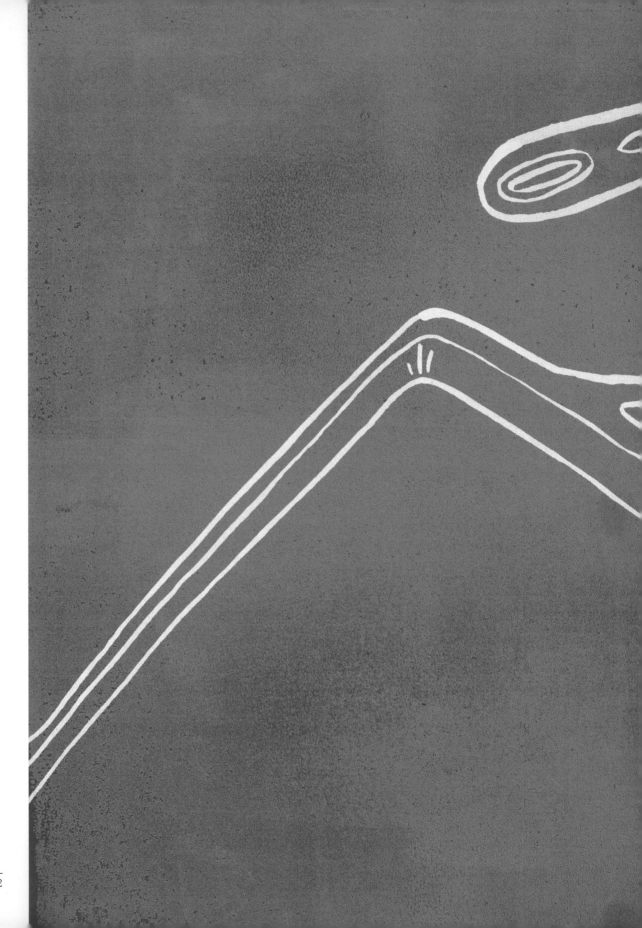

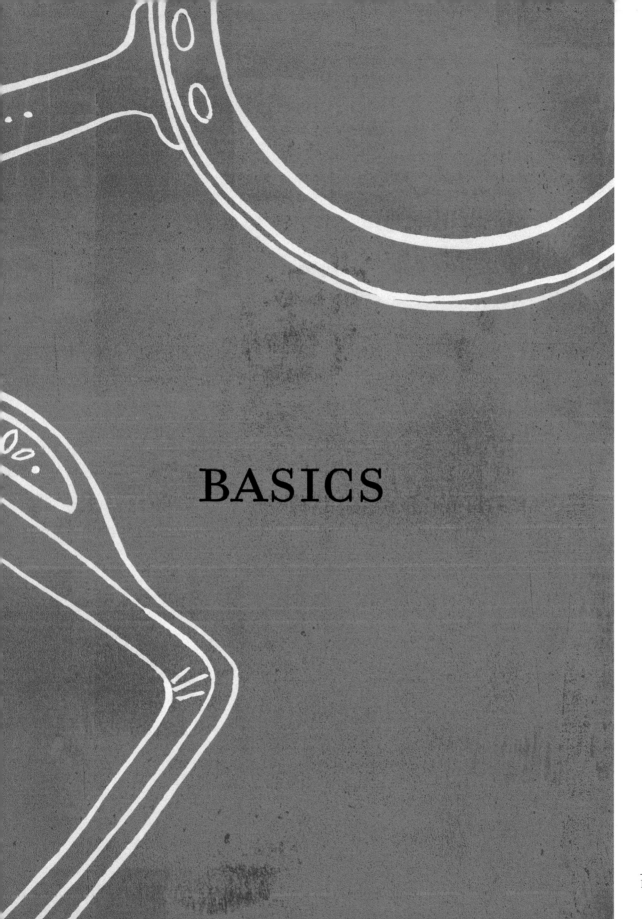

BASICS

300g (10oz) brown rice flour

50g (2oz) tapioca flour

40g (1½oz) potato flour

40g (1½oz) cornflour

Place all the flours together in a bowl and stir well.

Sieve the flours into a funnel placed in the neck of a storage jar. (This not only minimizes clumps, but also blends the mixture more fully.)

Store the flour blend for up to 1 month, or no longer than the earliest 'best before date' of the flours used.

Gluten-free Plain White Flour Blend

Most supermarkets or health-food shops sell gluten-free plain white flour blends (also known as gluten-free all-purpose flour blends) that are specially formulated to replace white wheat flour. These are usually very good, but if you can't find any or if you would rather make your own, here is my version, which I used for all the applicable recipes in this book. I often make a double batch if I'm doing a lot of baking. I store the flour in a clip-top jar.

MAKES ABOUT 280G (10OZ)

100g (3½oz) Gluten-free Plain White Flour Blend (see page 164)

55g (2oz) potato flour

½ teaspoon xanthan gum

¼ teaspoon gluten-free baking powder

pinch of salt

75g (3oz) cold unsalted butter, diced

60ml (2fl oz) water

In a food processor, pulse together the flour blend, potato flour, xanthan gum, baking powder, salt and butter for a few seconds until the mixture resembles breadcrumbs. Add the measurement water and blend briefly to form a sticky dough. Leave for a few minutes to absorb the water, then shape into a ball.

Alternatively, mix together the flours, xanthan gum, baking powder and salt in a bowl, add the butter and rub in using your fingertips until the mixture resembles breadcrumbs. Stir in the water, then knead for 1 minute until well combined – the mixture will seem ridiculously sticky, but gradually the flours will absorb the moisture and you'll be left with a soft dough.

Wrap the pastry in clingfilm and chill for 30 minutes – this makes it easier to roll out.

To blind bake a pastry case, preheat the oven to 180°C/350°F/ Gas Mark 4. Roll out the pastry to about 4mm (¼ inch) thick on a work surface well dusted with cornflour. Line a 20cm (8 inch) tart tin with the pastry and trim any excess using a sharp knife. Line the case with foil or baking paper, then fill with dried beans or ceramic baking beans. Bake for 30 minutes (or as specified by the recipe) until golden. Remove the paper and beans and leave to cool.

Plain Shortcrust Pastry

This is a very versatile shortcrust pastry that doesn't crumble when cooked, tastes great and can be rolled out very thinly. To be honest, it's even (whisper it) somewhat easier to make and use than standard pastry because there is no need to worry about it getting warm while you handle it and it doesn't shrink nearly so much during baking. It makes enough to line a 20cm (8 inch) tart tin or make 18 tartlets. You can also make double quantities so you can chill or freeze half for another time. See opposite for rich and sweet variations.

Rich Sweet Shortcrust Pastry

MAKES ABOUT 280G
(10OZ)

100g (3½oz) Gluten-free Plain White Flour Blend (see page 164)

55g (2oz) potato flour

½ teaspoon xanthan gum

¼ teaspoon gluten-free baking powder

1 teaspoon granulated sugar

75g (3oz) cold unsalted butter, cubed

1 egg

In a food processor, pulse together the flour blend, potato flour, xanthan gum, baking powder, sugar and butter for a few seconds until the mixture resembles breadcrumbs. Add the egg and blend briefly to form a sticky dough. Leave for a few minutes to absorb the moisture, then roll into a ball.

If you don't have a food processor, see opposite for an alternative method of making pastry – simply use an egg instead of the water.

Wrap the pastry in clingfilm and chill for 30 minutes – this makes it easier to roll out.

Sweet Shortcrust Pastry

MAKES ABOUT 280G
(10OZ)

100g (3½oz) Gluten-free Plain White Flour Blend (see page 164)

55g (2oz) potato flour

½ teaspoon xanthan gum

¼ teaspoon gluten-free baking powder

1 teaspoon granulated sugar

75g (3oz) cold unsalted butter, diced

60ml (2fl oz) water

In a food processor, pulse together the flour blend, potato flour, xanthan gum, baking powder, sugar and butter for a few seconds until the mixture resembles breadcrumbs. Add the measurement water and blend briefly to form a sticky dough. Leave for a few minutes to absorb the water, then roll into a ball.

If you don't have a food processor, see opposite for an alternative method of making pastry.

Wrap the pastry in clingfilm and chill for 30 minutes – this makes it easier to roll out.

MAKES 310ML (½ PINT)

1 tablespoon sunflower oil

20g (½oz) cornflour

250ml (8fl oz) milk

60ml (2fl oz) gluten-free
vegetable stock

1 bay leaf

¼ teaspoon gluten-free
ground nutmeg

Whisk together the oil and cornflour in a saucepan off the heat. Slowly whisk in the milk and stock until the mixture is lump-free, then add the bay leaf and nutmeg.

Place the pan over a medium heat and bring the mixture to the boil, whisking continuously until the sauce is thickened. Remove the bay leaf before using.

Béchamel Sauce

This is a quick and easy white sauce for use in a wide variety of dishes such as lasagne or cauliflower cheese. If you'd like a dairy-free version, use soya milk in place of the milk.

2 teaspoons olive oil

½ onion, finely diced

1 garlic clove, finely diced

2 x 400g (13oz) cans chopped
tomatoes

granulated sugar, to taste

2 teaspoons chopped fresh
herbs (optional)

salt and pepper

Heat the oil in a saucepan, add the onion and cook gently for 5 minutes until soft and slightly translucent. Add the garlic and fry for a further 1 minute.

Add the tomatoes and simmer, uncovered, for 20 minutes until thickened. Season with salt and pepper and add sugar to taste, then stir in the herbs, if using.

Simple Tomato Sauce

This very simple tomato sauce is perfect for serving with gluten-free pasta or with Swedish Meatballs (see page 82). Try it by itself, perhaps with a sprinkling of Parmesan, or flavour it by adding a couple of teaspoons of chopped fresh oregano, thyme or basil.

MAKES 310ML (½ PINT)

1 tablespoon sunflower oil

20g (½oz) cornflour

250ml (8fl oz) milk

60ml (2fl oz) gluten-free
vegetable stock

100g (3½oz) mature Cheddar
cheese, grated

Whisk together the oil and cornflour in a saucepan off the heat. Slowly whisk in the milk and stock until the mixture is lump-free.

Place the pan over a medium heat and bring the mixture to the boil, whisking continuously until the sauce is thickened. Add the cheese and cook, stirring, until the cheese melts. Use straight away.

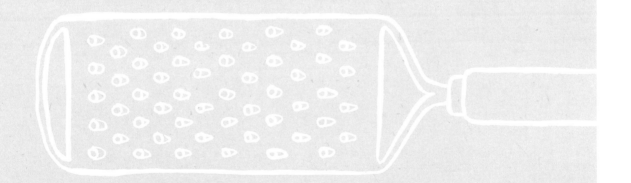

Cheese Sauce

This rich cheese-flavoured sauce is perfect poured over cooked gluten-free macaroni or steamed leeks. You can create a stronger flavour by using Bavarian smoked cheese instead of the Cheddar in this recipe.

SERVES 4

1 tablespoon cornflour

1 tablespoon olive oil

60ml (2fl oz) single cream

1 tablespoon grated horseradish

1 teaspoon lemon juice

Place the cornflour and olive oil in a saucepan over a medium heat and stir together until well mixed. Add the cream and cook, stirring, until the mixture starts to boil and thicken.

Remove the pan from the heat and stir in the horseradish and lemon juice. Leave to cool before serving.

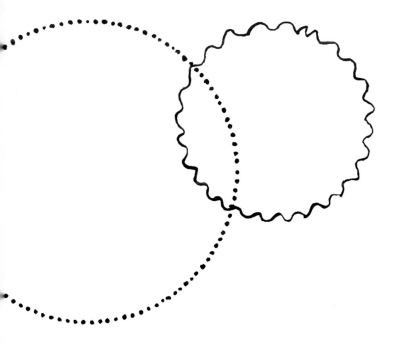

Horseradish Sauce

Some horseradish sauces contain added wheat flour, but luckily making your own is quick and easy. It is possible to buy grated horseradish preserved in vegetable oil, but you may even be able to find a fresh root. This sauce needs to be eaten on the day it is made. Serve with roast beef.

310ml (½ pint) water
1 tablespoon cornflour
salt and pepper

Pour 250ml (8fl oz) of the measurement water into the roasting tin after you have removed the cooked joint of meat or roasted bird and stir well to loosen all the baked-on bits.

Place the roasting tin directly on the hob, or transfer the mixture to a saucepan, and heat through. Strain off the fat. Sieve the gravy, if liked, and return to the pan.

Meanwhile, mix together the cornflour and remaining water in a cup until lump-free. Stir the mixture into the hot gravy and bring to the boil, stirring continuously until thickened. Season to taste with salt and pepper and serve.

Simple Gravy

Although most gravy granules contain wheat flour, you can also use cornflour to thicken gravy after cooking a joint or bird – here's how.

sunflower oil, for greasing

1 boneless pork chop, about 75g (3oz), fat trimmed and cut into 5mm (¼ inch) cubes

125ml (4fl oz) milk

2 dessert apples, about 200g (7oz) total weight, peeled, cored and finely chopped

2 teaspoons water

2 x 240g (8oz) cans whole chestnuts, drained and crumbled into small pieces

1 small onion, finely diced

1 egg, lightly beaten

2 teaspoons chopped parsley

pinch of salt

Preheat the oven to 180°C/350°F/Gas Mark 4. Grease a 1 litre (1¾ pint) pie dish with a little sunflower oil.

Place the pork in a saucepan, add the milk and simmer for 15 minutes until the meat is cooked through.

Meanwhile, put the apples and measurement water in a separate saucepan and cook over a low heat until softened, then drain.

Drain the pork, pouring 60ml (2fl oz) of the milk into a bowl (discard the rest), then add the pork, cooked apple pieces and all the remaining ingredients and stir well.

Spoon the mixture into the prepared dish and bake for 40 minutes until browned and crispy.

VARIATION
Make this stuffing dairy-free by substituting the milk with soya milk.

Chestnut & Apple Stuffing

This gluten-free stuffing is a firm favourite in our family where it is always served at Christmas. We almost prefer it to the roast meat it is served with! Although I suggest baking it in a pie dish, you could also use it to stuff a bird or joint.

300g (10oz) white Basmati or
other long-grain rice

750ml (1¼ pints) boiling water

Place the rice in a saucepan. Fill the pan with cold water and swoosh it about, then drain out the water. Add the boiling measurement water and cover with a tight-fitting lid.

Put the pan over a high heat and bring to the boil – as soon as the water bubbles, reduce the heat to its lowest setting and cook the rice for about 12–15 minutes (depending on the type of rice) until all the liquid has been absorbed.

Fluff up the rice with a fork and serve.

Perfect Rice

If there was one thing my mother drummed into me when I was a child, it was how to cook rice. This method leaves the rice perfectly tender without the need to drain (preserving many ofthe water-soluble vitamins) and without it becoming overly sticky either. The rule of thumb is 1 part rice to 2 parts boiling water. This makes everyday rice cookery dead easy: just find a receptacle that exactly holds the amount of dry rice you need, then fill it twice with boiling water. Add everything to your pan and away you go.

800g (1¾lb) red waxy potatoes, such as Desiree or Chieftain, peeled

160g (5½oz) potato flour, plus extra for dusting

¼ teaspoon gluten-free ground nutmeg

½ teaspoon salt

1 egg, lightly beaten

Cut the potatoes in half lengthways, then cut each piece lengthways into 3. Cook in a saucepan of boiling water for exactly 5 minutes, then drain and leave to cool completely.

Finely grate the cooled potato into a large bowl. Add the potato flour, nutmeg, salt and egg, then knead gently to form a soft but not sticky dough, adding a little extra potato flour if necessary.

Cut the dough in half, then each half into quarters. Roll out each piece of dough to a sausage about 2cm (¾ inch) wide on a work surface well dusted with potato flour, then chop into pieces about 2cm (¾ inch) long. You can leave the gnocchi like this, but if you want yours rounded, shape the pieces in the palm of your hand.

The gnocchi can be cooked immediately. Alternatively, dust with a little extra flour and refrigerate for a couple of days or freeze until needed.

To serve, drop the gnocchi into a saucepan of boiling water and cook for about 3 minutes – they will float when they are cooked through.

Gnocchi

The key to successful gnocchi is the variety of potato – you want a reasonably waxy variety for the best results. Serve with pesto or my Simple Tomato Sauce (see page 170) and a little grated Parmesan.

600g (1¼lb) large potatoes, peeled and cut into 2cm (¾ inch) pieces

50g (2oz) unsalted butter

40g (1½oz) potato flour, plus extra for dusting

½ teaspoon salt

Cook the potatoes in a saucepan of boiling water for 15 minutes until completely soft, then drain and return to the pan. Turn the hob off, then return the pan to the ring to allow any moisture in the potatoes to evaporate in the residual heat.

Add the butter and mash with a potato masher until smooth and lump-free. Add the potato flour and salt, then quickly knead into a slightly sticky dough. Cut the dough in half.

Using your hands or a rolling pin, shape each half of dough into a round about the size of a side plate and 1cm (½ inch) thick on a work surface well dusted with potato flour. Sprinkle both sides with potato flour.

Cook the rounds in a dry frying pan for about 5 minutes on each side until golden. Cut into quarters and serve hot.

Irish Potato Farls

These traditional, flat Irish potato cakes are almost bread-like when done. They make a great accompaniment to a breakfast of sausages, eggs and bacon, but they can also be enjoyed buttered and served with soup.

SERVES 2–3

2 tablespoons sunflower oil

1 celeriac, about 700g (1½lb)

2 garlic cloves, crushed

½ teaspoon gluten-free ground cinnamon

½ teaspoon cayenne pepper

½ teaspoon dried thyme

¼ teaspoon salt

¼ teaspoon ground black pepper

Preheat the oven to 180°C/350°F/Gas Mark 4. Pour the sunflower oil into a lipped baking sheet.

Using a sharp knife, chop away all of the tough outer edges and twisty root parts of the celeriac, leaving just the pithy centre. Slice this into 5mm (¼ inch) fingers.

Mix together the remaining ingredients in a large bowl, then add the celeriac fingers and toss until well coated. Spread the fingers out in the baking sheet and roll them around until coated in the oil. Bake for 20 minutes until browned and cooked through.

VARIATION

You can make plain celeriac fries by coating the celeriac fingers in a little oil and salt before baking.

Jerked Celeriac Fries

While celeriac is undeniably one of the ugliest vegetables around, it does have one major virtue: it's very low in carbohydrates (only about 9 per cent) and has various nutritional benefits. Here I've put celeriac to good use by turning it into a few portions of spicy fries.

250g (8oz) masa harina

375ml (13fl oz) water

½ teaspoon salt

Place the masa harina in a large bowl and add the measurement water and salt, then mix together to form a soft, pliable dough.

Heat a large, dry frying pan over a medium-high heat.

Cut down the sides of a large freezer bag, then take a ball of dough about the size of an egg and place it inside the cut bag. Create a thin, flat dough circle about the size of a side plate by rolling across the bag with a rolling pin (don't make the tortilla too thin or you won't be able to get it out of the bag).

Carefully peel off one side of the plastic bag, place your hand on top of the exposed tortilla and then flip the bag so the tortilla sits on your outstretched palm. Unpeel the rest of the bag and flip the tortilla into the hot pan.

Cook the tortilla for about 2 minutes on each side until it becomes patchily browned, then transfer to a plate, cover and keep warm in a low oven while you make and cook the remaining tortillas. Serve immediately.

Corn Tortillas

Traditional Mexican tortillas are made with a specially treated cornmeal, called masa harina. The treatment, known as nixtamalization, was developed thousands of years ago. It breaks down some of the internal structure of the maize and means the resulting flour is more nutritious and can be used in many more ways than standard cornmeal. One common use is in these thin and naturally gluten-free flatbreads. You may need to buy masa harina from a specialist store or online, but it's worth trying, especially if you enjoy Mexican food.

300g (10oz) Gluten-free Plain White Flour Blend (see page 164)

2 eggs, lightly beaten

4 teaspoons sunflower oil

250ml (8fl oz) milk

1 tablespoon granulated sugar

pinch of salt

2 teaspoons gluten-free baking powder

sunflower oil or butter, for frying

Place the flour blend in a bowl, add the eggs and oil and stir together. Pour in half the milk and mix together until smooth, then gradually stir in the remaining milk until it forms a thick batter. Leave to stand for 15 minutes, then stir in the sugar, salt and baking powder.

Meanwhile, smear the surface of a large frying pan with kitchen paper dipped in oil. Heat the pan over a medium-high heat until hot. Spoon dollops of batter into the pan and cook until the surface of the pancakes turns matt, then flip them over and cook for a further minute until golden brown. Transfer to a plate and keep warm in a low oven while you cook the remaining batter.

Pancakes

This recipe makes a good basic pancake, to be dressed up any way you wish: add some blueberries to the batter, and serve them with bacon and maple syrup.

MAKES ABOUT 20

225g (7½oz) Gluten-free Plain White Flour Blend (see page 164)

500ml (17fl oz) milk

2 eggs

2 teaspoons sunflower oil, plus extra for greasing if needed

1 teaspoon granulated sugar

½ teaspoon vanilla extract

pinch of salt

Place the flour blend and milk in a saucepan and cook, whisking continuously, until the mixture thickens. (This happens quite quickly and the mixture can become quite stiff, but don't worry about lumps at this stage and just whisk it as thoroughly as you can manage.) Remove the pan from the heat and leave to cool for about 5 minutes.

Add the remaining ingredients to the mixture then, using a hand-held blender or food processor, blend until smooth.

Heat a waffle iron on a medium setting. (If it's not nonstick, give it a light oiling before use.) Add a dollop of the batter and close the waffle iron. Cook according to the manufacturer's instructions until dark golden brown and cooked through. The waffles are best served hot.

Waffles

Waffles are one of life's simple pleasures – and this method eliminates grittiness. Try these simply dusted with icing sugar.

35g (1oz) brown rice flour

250ml (8fl oz) milk

250ml (8fl oz) water

55g (2oz) potato flour

pinch of salt

2 eggs, lightly beaten

sunflower oil or butter, for frying

Place the rice flour and milk in a saucepan and heat gently, whisking continuously, until the mixture thickens. Remove the pan from the heat and gradually whisk in the measurement water, then the potato flour and salt. Whisk in the eggs. Pour the batter into a jug.

Lightly smear the surface of a large frying pan with kitchen paper dipped in butter or oil. Heat the pan over a medium heat, then pour in a dollop of batter and swirl the pan so it forms a thin layer across the base of the pan. Cook for 2–3 minutes until golden underneath, then flip it over and cook for a further 2–3 minutes until spottily browned. Transfer to a plate and cover with a clean tea towel while you cook the remaining batter. Serve warm.

Crêpes

Super-thin yet robust French pancakes are possible with gluten-free flours – you just need to know the right method. These lacy crêpes do, however, take a little longer to fry than standard pancakes, so I recommend cooking them in a large frying pan. My favourite way to serve these is French-style with a little sugar, or lemon juice and sugar, but my kids would definitely say they prefer chocolate spread…

MAKES ABOUT 30

300g (10oz) buckwheat flour

2 teaspoons gluten-free baking powder

pinch of salt

2 eggs, lightly beaten

4 teaspoons sunflower oil

375ml (13fl oz) milk

sunflower oil or butter, for frying

Mix together the flour, baking powder and salt in a bowl, then stir in the eggs and oil. Gradually add the milk, stirring continuously until it forms a smooth batter.

Smear the surface of a large frying pan with kitchen paper dipped in butter or oil. Heat the pan over a medium-high heat. Using a tablespoon, drop 2 or 3 dollops of batter into the pan (make sure they're not touching) and cook for about 1 minute until bubbles form on the surface, then flip them over and cook for a further 1 minute or until golden brown. Transfer to a plate and keep warm in a low oven while you cook the remaining batter. Eat the same day.

Blinis

Blinis are savoury pancakes from Russia that are often made with buckwheat flour, which has a distinctive taste and is a rich source of minerals and vitamins. Though buckwheat is naturally gluten-free (it's actually the seeds of a plant related to rhubarb), the flour displays similar properties to wheat flour so making these pancakes is straightforward. Serve them hot or cold with soured cream, smoked salmon, lumpfish roe and chopped chives, or try them topped with egg mayonnaise and a sprinkling of cress.

55g (2oz) potato flour

40g (1½oz) icing sugar

40g (1½oz) soft dark brown sugar

½ teaspoon sunflower oil

¼ teaspoon vanilla extract

¼ teaspoon xanthan gum

60ml (2fl oz) water

Preheat the oven to 160°C/325°F/Gas Mark 3.

Mix together the flour, sugars, oil, vanilla extract and xanthan gum in a bowl. Gradually stir in the measurement water until smooth. Leave to stand for 10 minutes.

Using a pencil, draw round a 15cm (6 inch) diameter upturned bowl or side plate on nonstick baking paper to create 5 circles. Cut the circles out, leaving a border around the edge for you to hold.

Lay the paper circles on a baking sheet. Place a heaped tablespoon of the mixture into the centre of each circle, then spread it out evenly to the drawn line using a palette knife. Don't make the edges too thin and don't leave any holes. Bake for about 17 minutes until browned and hardened.

Carefully remove the discs from the oven, then quickly grab the edge of the paper using a tea towel or oven glove and roll the circle into a cone shape. Hold for a few seconds until the mixture cools enough to be handled; at this point you can peel off the paper and form a tighter cone, pinching the bottom to prevent ice cream dripping out. The cones are delicate, so be careful.

Transfer the cones to a wire rack, seam side down, and leave until completely hardened.

Ice Cream Cones

These crunchy cones require no special equipment and are just crying out for a dollop of luscious ice cream. The key to success is careful measurement of the ingredients. Store the cones in an airtight container until needed.

GLOSSARY

Here's a quick A–Z of different types of gluten-free flour and other more unusual ingredients you will find in this book.

BROWN RICE FLOUR

Both brown and white rice flours (also known as rice powders) are available. Both are made from ground rice and have a fine consistency. I choose brown rice flour because it contains extra nutrients and has more fibre than white rice flour (which is made from white/polished rice). Not to be confused with rice starch.

BUCKWHEAT FLOUR

Buckwheat is a relative of rhubarb and as such is naturally gluten-free. When buckwheat seeds are ground they produce a pale grey flour with a unique flavour.

CORNFLOUR

An ivory-coloured fine flour made from the starchy interior of maize; also known as corn starch. Not to be confused with cornmeal (see below).

CORNMEAL

Cornmeal is also known as maize meal or polenta – a coarse, yellow flour made from maize with the texture of fine breadcrumbs.

GLUTEN-FREE OATS

Oats carefully grown and processed to avoid gluten contamination.

GRAM FLOUR

Gram flour is also sold as besan, chickpea flour, chana flour or garbanzo bean flour. It is made from ground chickpeas and is very high in protein.

GROUND ALMONDS

Ground almonds is the name given to a coarse flour made from pure almonds – it may also be sold as almond meal or almond flour. For the recipes in this book, it doesn't matter whether you choose the kind that includes the skins of the almonds or not.

LINSEEDS

Also known as flaxseed, linseeds are the seeds of the flax plant. They may be brown or yellow and are a good source of fibre.

MASA HARINA

Masa harina is the name given to a special pale, fine cornmeal made from nixtamalized corn. Nixtamalization improves the nutritional content of the corn and also means the cornmeal will stick together and form a dough when liquid is added.

POTATO FLOUR

A white starch derived from potatoes, this makes a good thickening agent.

TAPIOCA FLOUR

Tapioca flour is a bright white starch made from the root of the cassava or manioc plant. It is very useful in gluten-free cooking because it goes very stretchy when mixed with liquid and heated.

XANTHAN GUM

Xanthan gum is a sticky substance produced by certain bacteria that is then dried to form a pale grey powder. It can be used for a variety of food-related uses. In gluten-free cooking it is most commonly used to help reduce crumbliness in cakes or pastry, or to provide elasticity to dough. I try not to use it any more than strictly necessary. It is also worth checking the source of the xanthan because the bacteria can be grown on a number of different mediums (for example, wheat or milk) and this may make it unsuitable for individuals highly sensitive to those products.

Index

Acknowledgements

AUTHOR'S ACKNOWLEDGEMENTS

Thanks to all those over the years who helped with the various aspects of this book – your feedback was invaluable and I really appreciate the time and effort you spent on my behalf. The list is too long to name everyone, but I'd particularly like to mention the guys in the office (you know who you are!), Allison MacFarlan, Andrea and Gordon Wood, Becky and Steve Boyd, Clare Mills, Felicia Parker, Gillian Randall, Helen Rossiter, Julie Wood, Karin Enskog-Ali, Kim Lankshear, Rose Lewis, Ruth Gillingham, Sanne Williams, Tania Fish, Trish Lorenz and Zoe Bailey. In particular, I must mention Allyson Bates and Lucie Roberts, my right-hand women!

To Richard, Stanley, Astrid, Torben, Jacky, Hannah, Phil, Mum and Dad I'd like to say thanks for your patience during my experiments.

Thanks to Eve White and her assistant Jack Ramm for their support and validation. Equally, I am extremely grateful to Fiona Smith for her friendly assistance in the early stages of this process; and Nell Card and Mina Holland at the *Guardian*.

To Stephanie Jackson and all at Octopus Publishing, thank you for working with me on this book. To Alex, Jaz, Kat, Siân, Liz and Max – it was a pleasure. Thanks to Nina Hertig at Sigmar London for loan of some of the plates.

Finally, to Anne Balme: I am so grateful to you for the many afternoons you spent in my kitchen chatting about gluten-free cookery (not that you had much choice – I talked about little else for months!). This book would never have been the same without you.

ABOUT THE AUTHOR

Susanna Booth is a passionate and inventive self-taught chef who specializes in creating recipes for specific dietary requirements. A former recipe columnist for the *Guardian*, she uses her degree in Polymer Chemistry to offer a fresh perspective on some of our best-loved dishes.

An Hachette UK Company
www.hachette.co.uk
First published in Great Britain in 2015
by Hamlyn, a division of
Octopus Publishing Group Ltd
Carmelite House
50 Victoria Embankment
London EC4Y 0DZ
www.octopusbooks.co.uk

Copyright © Octopus Publishing Group Ltd 2015
Text copyright © Susanna Booth 2015

ISBN 978 0 60063 042 5

A CIP catalogue record for this book is available from the British Library

Printed and bound in China

10 9 8 7 6 5 4 3 2 1

Publishing Director - Stephanie Jackson
Art Director - Jonathan Christie
Design - Jaz Bahra
Senior Editor - Alex Stetter
Ilustrations - Abigail Read
Photography - Haarala Hamilton
Home Economist and Food Stylist - Kat Mead
Nutritionist - Angela Dowden
Production Controller - Meskerem Berhane